The Flame
of the
Heart

TORKOM SARAYDARIAN

Visions for the Twenty-First Century®

The Flame of the Heart

© 1991 The Creative Trust

ISBN: 0929874-02-1

Library of Congress Catalog Number 91-92891

Printed in the United States of America

Cover design: *Fine Point Graphics*
Sedona, Arizona

Printed by: *Thomson - Shore, Inc.*
Dexter, Michigan

Published by: **T.S.G. Publishing Foundation, Inc.**
Visions for the 21st Century®
P.O. Box 7068
Cave Creek, AZ 85331-7068 U.S.A.

Note: The meditations and prayers contained in this book are given as guidelines. They should be used with discretion and after receiving professional advice.

O Lord of Beauty,
let me stand in Your Temple
of color supernal
and within the symphonies divine.
May I achieve harmony
with the Heart of the Cosmic rhythm
and radiate the uplifting,
expanding beauty of that Heart
in all my actions, aspirations, and visions.

M.M.

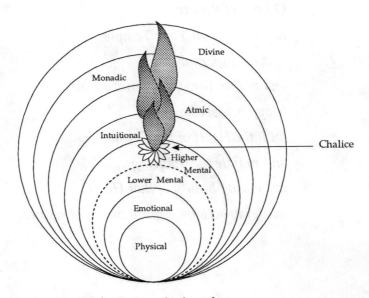

Divine

Monadic

Atmic

Intuitional

Chalice

Higher
Mental

Lower Mental

Emotional

Physical

The Flame of the Heart

Table of Contents

Diagrams

To behold with the eyes of the heart; to listen with the ears of the heart to the roar of the world; to peer into the future with the comprehension of the heart; to remember the cumulations of the past through the heart; thus must one impetuously advance upon the path of ascent. Creativeness encompasses the fiery potentiality, and is impregnated with the sacred fire of the heart. Therefore, upon the path to the Hierarchy, upon the path of Great Service, upon the path of Communion, synthesis is the one luminous path of the heart. How can the manifested rays be radiated if the flame is not affirmed in the heart? It is precisely the quality of the magnet that is inherent in the heart. The highest creativeness is imbued with this great law. Hence, each consummation, each union, each great cosmic unification is achieved through the flame of the heart. By what means can the foundation of the great steps be laid? Verily, only through the heart. Thus the arcs of consciousness are fused by the flame of the heart.

Thus, we shall keep in memory the beauteous attraction of the magnet of the heart, which links all manifestations. Verily, the silver thread that links the Teacher with the disciple is the great magnet of the heart. The union between Teacher and disciple affirms the essence of all evolutions.

Heart, para. 1.

A Few Words

This book is about the Heart, about the Core of our being in which there is the Life, there is our Essence, there is the Self.

Western civilization has cultivated the mind, and as a result we have a powerful technology which is growing year after year in a marathon race, leaving the heart far behind.

Most of the political conditions and economic problems of the world, as well as the problems in our families and societies, are based on the fact that our heart has been left behind; its whispers are not considered as safe advice, and they are easily neglected.

The heart was left behind because those who lived only through their heart became victims of exploitation and ridicule by those who had developed their mind. The latter could easily cheat and manipulate those who had heart but not a developed mind. Thus the mind lost a true guide in the heart, a guide who could help to create a more balanced and happy life in humanity.

When we refer to the heart, we do not mean the physical heart which pumps the blood, but to

— The center of motive within our being

— The inclusive quality of our Real Self

— The organ of pure sensitivity in our being

— Our pure consciousness

— The link between us and Cosmos

— The center of compassion and love within us

— The sense within us that feels joy and ecstasy when it records beauty in any form, sees virtues and experiences of heroic action and inclusive service

— The heart center which is found behind the physical heart, four to six inches away from our body, and is recognized as a twelve-petaled golden lotus

— The blue flame in the heart

It is from the heart that all the blessings of life, shared with all living beings, pour out.

We are told by a great Teacher that the heart is the most sensitive "organ." If it is alive and unfolding, it transmits life-giving energies. But if it is petrified, it turns into the cause of our destruction.

In the coming ages, the importance of the heart will be discovered all over the world. As we build universities to develop the mind, we will also build universities where the heart will be developed to balance the mind.

It is the balance of the heart and the mind that will lead humanity to a golden age.

The thoughts of people will be enlightened by the flame of the heart, and the heart will guide all

that the mind does, charging it with the vision of the future and with the light of all inclusive Purpose.
    M.M. says,

>...*Each consummation, each union, each great cosmic unification is achieved through the flame of the heart*....[1]

>...*The warmth of the sun and the warmth of the heart are our life-givers.*[2]

>...*The mightiest lever of Cosmos, and the most sacred, is the heart. Its consciousness fills Space; its light illumines Cosmos.*[3]

>...*How necessary it is to learn to feel one's heart not as one's own, but as the universal one....*[4]

This book is an effort to emphasize the importance of the heart in all our relationships with people and with all forms of life.

1. Agni Yoga Society, *Heart*, para. 1.
2. Agni Yoga Society, *Infinity*, Vol. I, para. 79.
3. *Ibid.*
4. Agni Yoga Society, *Heart*, para. 7.

The Heart

In the Ageless Wisdom, the *heart* refers to a golden twelve-petaled lotus located behind the physical heart about four to six inches away from the body. This heart can be found in various stages of development. Sometimes it is like a small bud. Sometimes only three petals are open. Sometimes the petals are hardened in varying degrees. Sometimes this heart is a fully developed, radioactive lotus.

The term *heart* also refers to motives. Real motives originate from the heart. Ninety percent of our decisions are made in the heart. The mind is just a laborer; it works and formulates, but the final decisions come from the heart. If the heart is pure, you will always make the right decision in any situation. In critical moments, especially, the heart interferes and overrides the power of reasoning and logic.

The term *heart* also refers to that central organ in our physical nature which is the distributor of energies throughout our system. Our physical heart is the replica of the corresponding hearts that we have on the emotional, mental, and Intuitional Planes. These hearts stand behind each other like reflections.

The emotional heart distributes compassion into our system. The mental heart distributes light energy. The intuitional heart distributes love energy. All of these energies are distributed into our system just as the physical heart distributes blood throughout the body. Each heart must be very healthy, strong, and integrated if we want the organs to receive the right energies from this central distributing system.

The term *heart* also refers to the sense which links all human beings and life forms in the world. For example, our physical heart connects us with the heart of the world. The heart of the world distributes the electromagnetic energies to all of Nature, pumping energy into the mineral, vegetable, animal, human, and angelic kingdoms.

The astral world also has a heart found on the astral plane. This heart controls the energies in the astral world. There is also a heart in the mental world, found on the mental plane, and a heart on the Intuitional Plane. The heart of man is sensitive to the activities of these hearts, and if man's heart is really open, he can register what is going on in the heart of Nature, the heart of the Subtle World, the heart of the Fiery World, and even the heart of higher realms.

Many people have the experience of feeling a pain in their heart, for unknown reasons, and later finding out that at that exact time a big earthquake or catastrophe was happening somewhere on the planet. Awakened disciples, whose hearts are sensitive and have bloomed, can register what is occurring on planetary levels. If the heart is more advanced, it can register what is happening on universal and Cosmic levels. This means that the heart is an organ which connects a person with the higher centers of distributing life energies.

In the future, human hearts will be observed to predict earthquakes. They are much more sensitive than our seismographic networks all over the world. A new science will be developed to monitor the movement of the earth through observing the human heart.

The concept of heart is an all inclusive concept. The heart is found in everything, in every

- atom

- cell

- form (vegetable, animal, man)

- planet

- solar system

- galaxy

The "heart" is a center in any system, and it continuously receives and distributes energy in that system to enable the system to follow the line of duties given to it by the Law of Evolution.

We are told that the direct flow of energy comes from

— The logoic twelve-petalled egoic Lotus in the Cosmic Mental Plane.

— The solar twelve-petalled Lotus.

— The planetary logoic Heart, also a twelve-petalled Lotus.

— The twelve-petalled human egoic lotus on the mental plane.

— The twelve-petalled heart centre in a human being.[1]

There are three Suns which give light to the whole Universe:

1. The Central Spiritual Sun, which corresponds to the Monadic essence in man

2. The Heart of the Sun, which corresponds to the Egoic Lotus

---

1.   Alice A. Bailey, *A Treatise on Cosmic Fire* (New York: Lucis Publishing Co., 1951), p. 1205.

3. The physical Sun, which corresponds to the heart center of man on the etheric plane

Ancients used to say that the path to the Most High is found through the heart. The human heart is the door leading to the path reaching to the Cosmic Heart. That is why the heart was considered the most sacred abode of the Most High.

Our schools have been devoted to studying the path of the mind. We do not know yet of any school dedicated to studying the Universe through the heart.

Thus, education has been related to the mind at the expense of the study and the education of the heart.

The culture of the heart was given in all great world Scriptures. We must dedicate our time to digging out the culture of the heart in these great Teachings and thus balance the mental teachings.

In this age of computers, it will not be too difficult to compile the culture of the heart. This culture must be systematized and, in a gradient scale, given to children in

— elementary schools

— high schools

— colleges

— universities

— spiritual schools

Our educational system has created mental giants, but without *heart culture*. These people are almost ready to destroy the life of this planet.

To balance the activities of these mental giants, we need the culture of the heart. Educated and transformed women can play the greatest role in formulating the science of the culture of heart, as by nature they have more sensitive hearts.

As our hearts are cultivated and unfolded, great changes will take place in our bodies, families, societies, nations, and in the world.

These great changes will occur due to the influence of the pure energies of compassion, love, and Intuition. Then all discoveries of the mind will be used to release the Divinity inherent in the human form.

Crime, horror, violence, revolutions, and wars — with all their equipment and "heroes" — will go to museums and be placed in a dark, sad corner.

One day, when I was visiting a museum with a friend and examining a sword that was ten feet long, my friend said, "One day that sword will be called 'shame.' " This friend died before the second war was ended. What would he think of the weapons which can destroy a city, an entire nation — even the planet!

Heart culture is the most urgent and essential element for the coming generations if we want them to survive on this planet.

There are five reasons why we should have a pure heart:

First, if you do not have a pure heart, you will never have joy, light, love, and energy. When you do something against your heart, you lose your joy, love, and enthusiasm. Many intellectual people cannot make the right decisions in critical moments of their lives because their heart is not pure. On the other hand, the most simple person, or a person in poverty, or one who has many physical weaknesses, can often make the right decision because of his pure heart.

A pure heart increases the light of your mind. A pure heart makes you able to enjoy whatever you have. You may sit before a table of the best food, but if your heart is not pure, the things you eat will turn into poison in your system.

This is why people pray before eating. Prayer purifies their heart to some degree so that when they eat they assimilate energy and become joyful and full of life.

Any time your heart is pure, you have a fearless attitude toward life. Something in a pure heart makes you stand and continue, no matter what happens. Strength comes from the heart.

2. Second, no one can take an initiation, expand his consciousness, or enter another level of consciousness or beingness without a pure heart.

Wisdom and beauty can only be assimilated by the heart. If you read a book with an impure heart, a heart full of jealousy, hatred, or anger, you will never understand the book in its real meaning, and there will be no response in you.

3. Third, contact with Higher Forces is impossible without a pure heart. A great Master once told someone, "I cannot contact you any more because there is a bad odor in your astral and mental bodies,

coming from the pollution of your heart." Many Great Ones, angels, and devas will not communicate with us when our heart is not pure. As a result, we lose our magnetic attraction with them.

Fasting is an outer phenomenon which reminds us that if we really want to communicate with higher beauties, ideas, and visions, we must be physically pure. Any impurity in the heart is an inflammable material which can ignite and cause damage in our systems when we contact Higher Forces. Many people who have tried to contact sacred places or higher centers were hurt or burned because of the combustible materials of impurity in their heart.

4.   Fourth, real creativity is impossible without a pure heart. Real creativity means to bring some beauty, some idea, vision, or revelation from Higher Realms to humanity.

Many artists write about the purification process they passed through in their lives. I was with a violinist once who came backstage before his performance and said that he could not perform because his heart was so full of anger toward a friend. His anger killed his inspiration.

Much so-called creativity is done because of business, money, and vanity, but real creativity is impossible without a purified heart. Without a pure heart your creativity has no power, it does not bring a message, and it does not build a true bridge through which you and others can ascend and transform yourselves.

5.   Fifth, you cannot increase your magnetism and success in the world unless you purify your heart.

Those who are successful in spreading beauty in the world are those who have a pure heart.

There are six elements that pollute the heart:

— fear

— anger

— hatred

— jealousy

— greed

— slander

When any of these six pollutants enter your heart, it becomes very difficult to purify it. People spend lives trying to purify their heart of these elements.

Once jealousy enters your heart, everything you read or hear will be contaminated with the emanations of jealousy from your heart. When you purify your heart of jealousy, you have greater understanding of other people. Understanding develops more and more as you purify your heart.

Greed fills your heart with the images of the things you want. These images fill your heart and eventually *block* it from receiving new light, new Intuition, and new beauties.

There are various dangerous states or conditions of the subtle heart which indicate something is wrong with it. One condition is seen as the *drooping petals.* Under the poison of negative emotions, the petals of the heart droop, just as the petals of a flower

droop when it is sprayed with a poisonous substance. The twelve petals of the heart correspond to
twelve virtues and when you act against one of the
virtues, the corresponding petal droops.

For example, there is a petal called *compassion*.
If you do not have compassion, if you start hating
people and doing criminal things, the compassion
petal droops, closes, decays, and eventually
vanishes. When any petal disappears in your heart,
it means that you are not in contact with one of the
corresponding energies of the Universe which gives
you life and which will eventually lead you to
higher levels of consciousness.

If you start exercising virtues, the petals of your
heart become lively and radiate energy into your
system. M.M. once said that any sickness, even cancer, can be cured by the energy of the heart.

Purification of the heart is necessary if you want
to use the energy of your heart for healing people.
If your heart is not pure, your efforts at healing will
have mixed results, and you will transmit both healing energy and poison. It is the heart that heals
people, but the heart will never be powerful unless
it is purified.

Another condition of the heart is called the state
in which the petals are *dried* and *petrified.* In the Agni
Yoga teachings, it says that the petrifying of the
petals of the heart is the greatest disaster for a
human being. There are three factors that really
petrify the petals of the heart:

— crime

— revenge

— separatism

Revenge petrifies the love petals of the heart and kills the sensitivity of the person so that he can even kill without feeling anything.

If you petrify your subtle heart, in future incarnations your physical heart will give you trouble in the form of heart disease, heart attacks, etc.

Another condition of the heart has to do with *blockage* of the energies of the heart. This blockage occurs when your motive is not pure. For instance, you have a great love for someone, but behind that love lie your self-interest and vanity. If the motive behind your love is not pure, your love energy cannot flow out to others; it is blocked within your heart, where it creates congestion with various physical repercussions.

In the near future, science will prove the existence of one hundred to two hundred different heart diseases, each one caused by various negative emotional and mental conditions. For example, self-pity is actually a disease of the heart. Hatred is a disease of the heart. These diseases will eventually be researched and carefully indexed.

Darkening of the heart is another condition of the heart. Normally the heart glows with a blue, fluorescent flame surrounded by twelve golden petals. If the heart traps impure thoughts — thoughts of hatred, crime, separatism, revenge, jealousy, and greed — the light of the heart darkens.

The next condition is called *conflict* within the heart. This condition is often created by post-hypnotic suggestions consciously or unconsciously controlling you, while the heart feels they are not right. Conflict in the heart causes irregularity and dishar- mony in the distribution of energies into the physi- cal, emotional, mental, and intuitional bodies, causing a great turmoil in your life.

You cannot hurt any human being without first damaging or ruining your own heart.

One day three people came to Christ and wanted to kill Him. But after they heard Him talk, they changed and eventually became His disciples. The beauty and purity of the heart of that Great One eventually created some kind of purification in their hearts, and they saw the evil in their intentions and motives.

The next condition of the heart is a state in which *past memories of pains and sufferings* continuously echo within your heart. This is a very dangerous state of the heart because it eventually destroys your blood and nervous systems. The best remedy for this condition is forgiveness. Forgiveness wipes out such painful memories.

There are ten methods you can use to purify your heart:

1. Overcome selfishness. Do not live just for yourself. Do not use other people for your own interests. Do not manipulate people. Selfishness is a world epidemic today, and with such a widespread epidemic we cannot really expect better world con- ditions than we have.

Relations between nations will never improve until we purify our heart of selfishness. No social, political, or economic condition will improve until the leaders of these activities purify their hearts. The people who have pure hearts can only be elected by those who have pure hearts. The conditions of the world can be changed only by those who have pure hearts.

2. Clean your vanities. Vanities distort the pure images you have in your heart. You must find exactly what you are, not more or less than what you are, so that you maintain balance, sanity, and equilibrium. The heart is the organ that brings equilibrium to your life.

3. Check your motives. You cannot clean your heart until you find the motives behind your actions, feelings, and thoughts. Your motives will reveal to you what is really going on in your heart.

Once you purify your heart, you will have cosmic energy within you. M.M. says that we communicate with Cosmos through our heart. We are initiated with our heart, and we conquer with our heart. Without a pure heart, we become a polluting factor in the world.

4. Develop the spirit of worship, aspiration, devotion, admiration, and a life dedicated to higher ideals. Aspiration means to find some beauty and try *to be* that beauty.

One day Rabindranath Tagore and his father were taking a boat ride on a lake. It was sunset, and the light was casting a beautiful reflection against a tree near the lake. Suddenly Tagore's father stopped the boat, and looking at the tree and the setting sun, the colors and the serenity, he began to fuse with the beauty in great ecstasy. That moment was an unforgettable joy in the heart of young Tagore.

5. **Renounce your ego.**

6. **Do not obsess and possess people.**

7. **Do not try to control the lives of others.** You can speak about the Teaching to others, but then you should leave them free to do anything they want to do, to live their own lives and learn from their own experiences. When the heart is purified, every kind of religion, ideology, and philosophy is synthesized, and you do not need to force people to change.

8. **Do not speak evil.**

9. **Try to see beauty in everyone.**

10. **Obey your heart.** This is the most important step of all. Always try to obey your heart...because God speaks through your heart.

There are other factors that damage the heart, and if you want to have an unfolding heart, you must know about them as well:

1. Sound, audible and inaudible, has a very strong influence upon the heart.

2. Mechanical sound, by which we are bombarded day and night on earth and from the

sky, will eventually make the human heart very weak.

3. Electrical currents, ELF waves (extremely low frequency), hurt the heart chakra.

4. Insecticides, various kinds of paint and varnish devastate the nerves connected with the heart. All chemical products, which fill our stores, printing shops, and paint stores, are detrimental to the heart.

5. Radioactive elements, fall-outs, gradually will harm the heart of humanity to an incurable degree.

The heart in our chest is linked and fused with the electromagnetic heart center in the etheric body. Both share each other's condition. They also affect the heart center in the head, which controls the mental behavior of man and the whole immune system. This is why Sages throughout history advised us to protect our heart.

Noise pollution has a deeper effect on our heart than chemical pollution. Noise pollution affects our etheric and astral heart centers and creates disturbances in the circulatory system of psychic energy, disturbing our etheric and astral health conditions.

All kinds of pollution are detrimental to our health, but especially noise pollution.

If possible, have as little noise in your home and office as possible. Stay at least five miles away from radio and television towers. Do not live on streets where the traffic is heavy, day and night. Especially, stay away from the vicinity of airfields.

These precautions will help you have a good and healthy heart.

*The Twelve
Energies of the Heart*

Physiologically, psychologically, and esoter-
ically, the heart is the central organ in man.

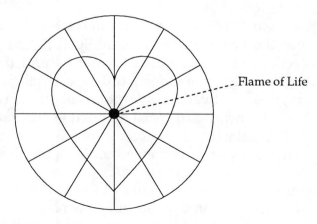

The Etheric Heart Center

There is the heart, and behind it there is an electromagnetic energy field with twelve flames originating from the center of the heart. The center is the foundation of life, originating from the Self, from the Spark. The Transcendental Self and the center of the heart are connected by the silvery thread which in the Ageless Wisdom is called the *life thread*.

The Transcendental Self, in Its turn, is a beam of life emanating from the Cosmic Heart. We have a Global Heart, which is the Hierarchy. We have a Solar Heart, which is the Heart of the Sun. We have a heart at the center of our galaxy, the Galactic Heart, and another heart is found beyond our galaxy.

Actually, the human heart is connected with these hearts by the silver thread; and when the heart is purified, it registers the events going on in the Global, Solar, Galactic, and Cosmic Hearts. Our heart registers earthquakes, explosions, calamities, and disasters occurring on the earth, in the solar system, and even in the galaxy.

Most of the time man is unaware of these things, but the heart registers them. Such registration affects the electromagnetic center behind the heart, and the heart manifests different rhythms, pains, anguish, and various symptoms of ailments.

The heart also registers great events on global, solar, galactic, and Cosmic planes, for example: when a group of advanced souls passes through an initiation; when Great Ones advance and are admitted into higher planes of Cosmos; when evil is defeated on some plane, or a new plane succeeds in cooperating on a Cosmic scale; when a new light and a new revelation emerge from Cosmic sources. The heart rejoices at these events. The heart registers them, although it is only in rare moments that the brain is aware of the registration of the heart. If a galaxy is in the process of disintegration, the heart registers it. If a new galaxy is in formation, the heart registers it as well.

The heart also records the emotions, thoughts, and plans of our friends. If they are sending benevolent thoughts, the heart rejoices. If they are sending negative thoughts, the heart feels the burden.

So often our moods are direct echoes of thoughts and emotions sent to us. We can uplift people through our pure and best thoughts, or we can cause them pain and suffering through our uncontrolled and wild thoughts and emotions.

We are told that there are seven sacred energies which are passing through the zodiacal signs and through our Sun, bringing to our solar system and our globe a flood of light, love, and power. The human heart is the assimilator of these energies, and if the consciousness of man begins to function on more refined levels, these energies will be used as communication lines — between man and the sources of the energies — through the human heart.

Every organization and every group has its own heart. The heart is a mechanism which receives, assimilates, and transmits life energies to keep the forms in line with the Purpose of life and to reveal the Purpose of life. Each heart translates the same Purpose in different magnitudes, according to the unfoldment and level of the heart.

In the human heart these seven cosmic energies are assimilated and changed into twelve radiations or twelve streams of energy. These are

1. The energy which heals

2. The energy which gives serenity and peace

3. The energy which gives joy and leads us into sacrificial service

4. The energy which gives courage, daring, striving, and patience

5. The energy which gives love, unification, and inclusiveness

6. The energy which causes universalism and synthesis

7. The energy which evokes beauty

8. The energy which creates understanding, timelessness, straight knowledge, and Intuition

9. The energy which records

10. The energy which enables us to receive great inspirations and become creative

11. The energy which transmutes

12. The energy which changes into righteousness and compassion[1]

The first energy of the heart heals. Watch children when they fall down or hurt themselves. They run to their mother and put their head on her heart, and they feel peace and security. If someone is in fear, in trouble, confused or grieving, take his head and embrace it on your heart in silence. Watch what will happen.

I remember a lady who had lost her two daughters. She was in a desperate condition while everyone around her was trying to comfort her with no result. Knowing the power of the heart, I approached her, pulled her head to my heart, and kept it there for a few minutes in silence. When I lifted her head, she opened her eyes and said, "I guess it was God's Will. I feel all right. I think I can overcome my grief. As you were holding my head, I began to think about the continuity of life on other planes and about Infinity...."

I did not answer her but smiled, and she continued, "I knew there was a better way to comfort myself than with pills."

Once we learn how to channel the healing energy of the heart, we become unseen healers, and we heal people on the physical, emotional, and mental planes.

---

1. For further information on twelve energies of the Chalice, please refer to *The Science of Becoming Oneself*, Chapter 12, "The Chalice and the Seeds." See also *The Science of Meditation*, Chapter 24, "Twelve Stages of Illumination."

The healing energy of the heart harmonizes the rhythm of the body and creates rhythm and harmony in the functions of the glands through the centers.

The heart center controls the other six centers in the etheric body. The impulse of an unfolded and purified heart goes through each center and synchronizes and regulates it. When your centers are synchronized and regulated through the rhythm of the heart, the glands and the corresponding organs are regulated.

Health starts and ends with your heart. When your heart is taken by someone, your whole being is taken. When your heart is broken, your whole being is broken. It is the heart that is the fortress of your being.

At the center of the heart there is a flame. It is the Flame of Life. And it is this Flame that transmutes the energies of the seven streams and changes them into the twelve energies of the heart. These twelve energies are the sources of the twelve most essential minerals of your body, emotions, and mind. Through these minerals the heart repairs, cures, and regenerates the organs.

It is this Flame that transmits psychic energy to the man. Psychic energy is the synthesis of the seven Cosmic and twelve heart energies. Psychic energy is the healing energy which cures, enlightens, purifies, regenerates, and puts man in tune with the Will of the Almighty Center of Life.

When the flame of the heart is gone, the degeneration of a person starts and his body, emotions, and thoughts show signs of deterioration. It is the flame of the heart that holds the whole man together in harmony with Cosmos. When the flame is gone, the ability to understand disappears.

The first help for healing must be evoked from the Heart Center of the planet, which in esoteric literature is called the Hierarchy. The Hierarchy is the source of psychic energy, which is the energy that makes all things new and regenerates the whole system of our vehicles, starting from the *consciousness*. The consciousness of man must change before true healing can take place.

Thus, the contact with the Hierarchy must be sought with great striving, labor, and invocation. Once the contact is established, psychic energy infiltrates our system and purifies, strengthens, and transforms it. Many miraculous healings happen at the moment of contact with the Hierarchy.

In case of illness or disease, the first step is to polarize your whole being toward the Hierarchy and try to establish a contact with that great Center of healing energy. The contact can be felt as an electrical energy filling your head, your heart, and your entire physical, emotional, and mental systems. On the physical level, the contact creates warmth, fragrance, light, color, etc. On the emotional plane, it creates profound peace and a feeling of release. On the mental plane, it creates enlightenment and generates a creative force. Enlightenment can reveal the causes of disease and challenge you to correct them; it also reveals the steps to be taken after the healing is accomplished so that the disease will not recur.

Prayers are efforts to contact the Hierarchy. Meditation is an effort to translate contacted energies. Sacrificial service is proof that one has contacted Hierarchy.

The Hierarchy is called the "primary remedy." Future health can only be secured through psychic energy, which is released at the time the man contacts his Soul and the Hierarchy.

The heart has a great healing quality. The heart center in man has a blue-orange flame which, when it is fully developed, turns into a mechanism of accumulation of Cosmic energies and a mechanism of distribution of these energies into our system, into our environment, and into far-off locations. The formation and blooming of the fire of the heart is carried out through sacrificial service and through exercising spiritual virtues in our lives.

It is in this flame that the received Cosmic energies fuse, and it is in this flame that the expansion of consciousness takes place. The Cosmic energies fuse and gradually form a rainbow-like sphere around the heart and even around the body, extending ten to fifteen feet. This is the sphere of energy which heals, uplifts, transforms, and enlightens people. All of one's words, thoughts, emotions, and actions carry the energy of this sphere to whomever or to whatever it is directed. This energy of the heart senses Cosmic events, and as the flame increases and develops purer colors, the whole sphere of the heart energy merges with the psychic energy in Space.

We are told that Christ, having reached such a state of unfoldment of the heart, could heal people

with His touch and with His thoughts. He was able
to establish contact with the Cosmic Heart.

It is the state of the hearts all over the world that
conditions international events and planetary disturbances or brings great harmony, health, and culture. We are told that this planet is protected by
great Hearts. The grouping of these Hearts is called
the Hierarchy of the planet. It is this Center that is
the source of all healing rays for our physical, emotional, and mental disturbances, as well as global
disturbances, disorders, or sicknesses. That is why
we are told to contact not only our heart, but also the
Planetary Heart for healing, enlightening, and
transforming our being.

The second energy gives serenity and peace.
The energy of serenity and peace expresses itself
through all that a man does. It is in serenity and
peace that the path toward the mystery of life is
found. This second energy emanates from the heart
and passes peace and serenity to people around the
person.

Peace and serenity make a man bloom and
flower. In olden times when they used to say
"peace" to each other, they put their hand on their
heart. One must be pure in heart to feel the existence
of the energy of peace and serenity of the heart.

Your heart always registers this energy of peace,
but your mind fails to register it and be conscious of
it. The reason for this is that there is no contact yet
between the heart and the mind. People must
develop this alignment between the brain, the mind,
and the heart if they want to enjoy the functions of
the heart. The heart registers the most distant events,

but if the mind does not translate the registrations, man remains unconscious of them. The great mystery of the Universe is revealed in the heart, but the brain-oriented man does not see that mystery.

The heart reflects the glories of the Universe. The mind translates the glories on its own level, through its contacts and its own interests.

When the mind is coordinated and works under the power and supervision of the heart, it turns into a creative source of service and becomes aware of the experiences of the heart and participates in them.

The third energy of the heart is joy and sacrificial service. The heart radiates joy. If the mind is not coordinated with the heart and does not work in harmony with it, it will never experience joy.

Joy is an energy which expands your beingness and gives you freedom. It releases you from limitations. The heart needs to be pure in order to radiate joy.

Joy releases you from your emotional and mental hindrances. Joy uplifts you. Joy expands you, purifies your mind, liberates you from your personality limitations, and lifts you to the level of the Transpersonal Self. When you reach the Transpersonal Self, you feel ecstasy. The Spiritual Triad, which is formed by light, love, and power, acts as a heart center in the higher planes. When your awareness is lifted into that center, you are in ecstasy.

Joy is the mastery of circumstances and the ability to radiate and clean the pollutions in your aura.

The third energy of the heart also inspires sacrificial service. The heart is concerned with the well-being of others before it thinks about its own well-being.

The average man thinks, speaks, feels, and acts based on his own personal interests. He feels that the world exists for him, and he must use the world for his personal interests. A noble man thinks he exists for the world. He is there to be useful to the world, and he tries to improve himself in any way possible to render greater service to others, meeting their needs on various levels. Sacrificial service works to bring great joy to others, even if the labor brings deep sorrow, tension, or pain.

The mind says, "How can I use this man or this object?" The heart says, "How can I be useful to people and use objects to help them?" The mind says, "That person has come to ask for help. He is lazy; he does not like me; let him learn to work and support himself." The heart says, "I know all this, but the man needs my help. He is me. I will help him in such a way that his needs are met and he is helped to meet his needs in the future."

In sacrificial service, you let the divine energy flow through you without being caught by your illusions, glamors, and self-interest. In sacrificial service, you do not even notice that you are doing something very important.

The fourth energy of the heart is the energy which gives you courage, daring, striving, and patience. It is this energy of the heart that inspires you to have courage and daring and challenges you to strive and transcend your level of beingness.

Sometimes, instead of relating yourself to your brain and expecting guidance from it, relate yourself to your heart and listen to its silent voice.

Try also to think in the heart instead of in the mind. Talk from the heart; watch from the heart; listen from the heart, and you will see what you were missing in your life. When you begin to talk the language of the heart, you will inspire people to do courageous things because when you speak through the heart you will build a communication line between your heart and the Heart of the Universe. You will inspire people with the vision or idea of limitlessness, with the vision of transcendental values, with the vision of Infinity — and that creates courage. You will raise people from their failure image toward their image of victory.

We are continuously impressed and superimposed by our failure image when we fail, when we are reminded of our past failures. We are reminded when people around us, such as our parents, teachers, ministers, friends, and bosses continuously emphasize the failure image in us.

Heart energy, when activated, destroys these images and wipes them out. It releases you, brings you out of your prison, and makes you realize that there is hope, there is success, there is a future for you. It makes you feel that there is an infinite heart, the *Abode*, a Cosmic Heart where you receive refuge, glory, and power.

You can reach and contact the Cosmic Heart through your own heart.

The energy of courage, daring, striving, and patience is a stream of energy which comes from your heart.

The mind calculates, acts as a compass, and bases its activities on past experiences and data. But the heart dares, has courage, and strives toward the future. The mind says, "A human being can do things according to the abilities he develops." The heart says, "A man can do almost anything if he dares." The mind says, "You can't." The heart says, "There is every possibility within you; you can."

Heroes are not the flowers of a mental plant but the flowers of the heart. One moment of contact with the stronghold of the heart makes you a hero. Those who obey the whisperings of their heart are on the path of heroism.

The mind says, "If you follow your heart, you may lose money, time, energy, and maybe popularity." The heart says, "Do it in the light of solemnity, beauty, and selflessness." All great things that are done in this world are motivated by the heart. All "great things" created by the mind without the blessings of the heart will be burdens on the shoulders of humanity or hindrances on the path of its transformation.

Patience is a subjective sense which feels Eternity, Infinity. In patience one identifies himself with the infinite domain and sees things in the light of millenniums. Things do not bother such a person. Patience is achieved when the failures, mistakes, and crimes of others do not irritate the person any longer because he detaches himself from the three lower worlds.

**The fifth energy of the heart is the energy of
love, unification, and inclusiveness.** It can also be
called the energy of unification, the energy of synthesis. It is the heart that unifies; it is the heart that
synthesizes.

The absence of love energy creates separatism,
hatred, and aggressive selfishness. The mind feeds
these things and eventually creates a psychological
isolation in man. The energy of the heart melts them
away and brings people closer to each other; it
creates fusion and synthesis.

People are used to looking at each other through
their brain and mind. Once you start looking at the
world and at people through your heart, you will
not believe the difference.

Looking through your heart, you feel your kin-
ship with all that exists. You feel the bliss of synthesis; you feel the oneness of all that exists. It is this
condition that burns away all the roots of future pain
and suffering and heals the cleavages between you,
nature, and people. Sickness and disease are the
result of cleavages. Every effort to heal cleavages is
an effort for everlasting health, harmony, and bliss.

Once a couple came to me for counseling. The
man said, "I hate that woman."

And the woman said, "I also hate him. I *hate*
him!"

"Well," I said, "if you want me to help you, you
must do whatever I suggest to you. Will you?"

They both answered "Yes."

"Put your right hand on your heart and feel the
beat. Close your eyes and relax and feel the heart.
Then visualize two eyes in your heart. When you

really visualize this, open your physical eyes and look at each other as if you were looking at each other through the eyes of your heart."

Five minutes later they opened their eyes and began to look at each other as if they were strangers. Then they smiled; then joy filled their faces; then they approached and hugged each other. The man said, "You know honey, I always loved you."

"And I always wanted you to tell me that you love me."

"But do you love me?"

"Are you kidding? Yes." Then they kissed each other. I saw the miracle of heart energy.

You must learn to relate through the heart, think in the heart, speak by the heart and to the heart, and you will see how much time and distance is saved.

It takes very little effort to learn this method. Try to exercise thinking, feeling, speaking, and observing through your heart.

When we are referring to the heart we are not referring to emotions and feelings; we are referring to a center where the twelve heart energies put man in contact with the Heart of the Universe.

The heart center is the furnace in which knowledge changes into love-wisdom. Love-wisdom connects a man with the Heart of the Sun. Love nourishes the core of your etheric centers and integrates them with the rhythm of your heart. A synchronization takes place in your being through love. If you love people, your love increases and performs miracles. If other people love you, their love nourishes your creative fires.

When you are stable in your love to people, your love becomes a path of transformation for them, and in their darkest hours, your love uplifts and encourages them toward new summits.

True love emanates from the Intuitional Plane, which is the Fourth Cosmic Ether. It is this love that penetrates your whole personality at the time when the higher ether replaces the lower ether.[2] Your physical love becomes pure, your emotional love radiates without glamor, and your mental contacts become inclusive and universal. Let us not forget that the substance of love underlies all that exists and is the prime conductor of communication and contact.

Thus love unifies you, synthesizes you, and creates a symphony between different notes, beings, and existences. This is the love that emanates from the Fourth Cosmic Ether, or from the Intuitional Plane.

Once a girl asked me, "Isn't hatred an energy, and can't we use it?" The answer is this: Hatred is the wrong use of energy. It is the motive behind the use which makes an energy either love or hatred.

Hatred is the distorted use of energy. Love is energy, the only energy that underlies all other energies or forces. When energy is used intentionally to separate, to exploit, to destroy, to enslave, to humiliate, to rob, to steal, to reject, to paralyze, to

---

2. For additional information regarding this process, please refer to *Other Worlds*, Chapter 60; *The Science of Becoming Oneself*, pp. 80, 96; and *The Science of Meditation*, pp. 52-53.

refuse others the right of existence, we say a man is distorting energy because energy *is one.* Any attempt to misuse it in separative functions creates chaos.

The Universe is built upon the laws of symphony, upon the laws of synthesis. Any distortion of this symphony creates serious karma for the distorter. Hatred is an effort to distort this symphony; that is why hatred is the source of all misery, pain, and suffering in the world. Of course, hatred is not permanent because hatred makes a circle and destroys itself. Hatred is self-destructive. Suffering means you are doing something wrong against the symphony, harmony, and rhythm of the Universe.

The heart really senses when a person is approaching you with love or hatred. The heart feels an anguish, a pain, or a tension in the presence of the force of hatred.

Hatred burns the heart. Hatred nourishes fear. Those who hate are controlled by fear, and fear is the destroyer of the heart. Future medicine will operate on metaphysical levels because the roots of all physical and psychological problems originate there.

Hatred distorts the rhythm of the intake of prana and affects the spleen, heart, and lungs. Then it weakens the mind and the brain. Hatred is not a principle; hatred is a distortion. It distorts your synchronization with the greater centers of the Universe. Love exists. Hatred does not exist; we create it. Sickness is not a principle; it is a distortion of harmony and rhythm.

Anger has a very close affinity with hatred and fear. Anger is the process of release of the forces accumulated by hatred and fear. Anger focuses these forces for destructive purposes. Anger damages the heart and burns the subtle counter-parts of the nerves in the etheric body, which are called *nadis.*

Hatred, fear, anger, jealousy, and greed can be annihilated when love is restored in your system. When these five monsters are wiped out, your whole mechanism resumes its state of synthesis, health, and beauty. This is why we must learn to love more, to understand more, to appreciate more. All that Christ taught is deep psychology. His words are formulas of health. *"Love each other as I loved you."* Can anyone surpass such a formula?

People think that development means the in-crease of data and knowledge in their brain and mind. This is wrong. The growth of your mental body is not a sign of the unfoldment of your Essence, just as the growth of the body of a child does not reflect the growth of his mind if he has a retarded mind. Most of humanity now has a growing mind but with a retarded spirit within it. That is why the whole of civilization and culture is in danger.

In the East they say that Satan knows every-thing. But his wealth of knowledge does not make him an angel or a beneficent force in the Universe. It is not knowingness that makes you proceed on the path of your perfection, but your beingness; the transformation and transfiguration of your being-ness takes you forward on the path of perfection.

When the twelve energies of your heart are in operation, we say you are blooming, but if they are not cultivated and in operation, all your knowledge works against your own interest and survival. We must be more than blind not to see this in our contemporary civilization.

The liberation of humanity is through the heart.

We must remember also that the hateful thoughts of others pierce the aura of the heart like pins and weaken it. If someone really hates you, he can change the beat of your heart and create disorders in it. Such thoughts are called in the Ageless Wisdom, "poisonous arrows."

Thus one must create friends.

The energy of love also creates group love. Group love is the love we have for each other which enables us to achieve a great goal and render a great service to help others in such a way that the Purpose is achieved and the vision is actualized.

The individuals within a group do not need to relate on personality levels or for personality interests such as money, sex, food, etc. There is no personality reaction, gossip, criticism, or using others for one's own personal interest.

The group cannot exist unless it has a living purpose which is progressive and in harmony with the Plan. It is from the group love that the urge to serve is released.

Service is an energy which

— awakens your fires

— creates the urge toward beauty

— makes you stand on your feet

— allows you to work for the Plan

This energy of the heart also produces inclusiveness. Inclusiveness is the ability to respond to the essential Self, to respond to Beauty, Goodness, and Truth in any form, in any expression of life.

Our emotions and thoughts can be exclusive, but our Intuition and true love can only be inclusive. Inclusiveness expands our consciousness and expands the field of our experience. As one becomes inclusive, he develops the ability to assimilate more of the various elements with which he is coming in contact. Thus he enriches his intellectual, moral, and spiritual system with various elements. Exclusiveness deprives us of those elements which we need for growth and for maturity.

If you have a heart — a clean, pure, unfolding, blooming heart — you are inclusive. Some people do not have a heart; they have the organ, but the spirit is not there. These are dead hearts. A dead heart lives only for himself. The most dangerous persons on this planet are those who have a dead heart because a dead heart is a cave of hatred, revenge, depression, and indifference to the feelings of others, and it is a place where the germs of all crimes develop. Actually the heart degenerates and dies without the spirit of inclusiveness.

The sixth energy of the heart creates a sense of universalism and synthesis within you. Because of this energy you do not consider yourself as the center of the universe, but you become progressively more inclusive. You no longer live for your ego or self-saturated life, running after your self-interest, but you accept the Infinite and feel like a part of It.

This sixth energy gradually destroys all separatism, all self-interest, all ego, and makes you a citizen of the Universe. This energy puts you in contact with Solar and Galactic Hearts to such a degree that all your thoughts, emotions, words, and actions express universalism and work for the benefit of all creation.

In essence, the whole existence is one great Entity. It is a Being. There are no cleavages in It. It is synthesis. The sixth energy of the heart helps man to see this synthesis in the artificial cleavages that man created through his ego.

This energy uplifts you from the limitation of your physical, emotional, and mental consciousness, which is separative in its nature, and puts you into the consciousness of the Transcendental Self. This is the True Self within. *"More radiant than the Sun, purer than the snow, subtler than the ether is the Self, the spirit within my heart. I am that Self. That Self am I."* The *Upanishads* clearly indicate that the Self is within the heart.

Of course, the head, the brain, and the mind are very important mechanisms. But they, as a whole, are the typewriter upon which the heart types, or should type, its visions. The brain will never understand the subtleties of life. Only the heart can understand, and Intuition awakens through the heart.

This sixth energy develops the sense of synthesis through which one sees the future perfection and the continuous refinement of forms and fusion with their prototypes.

The seventh energy of the heart evokes beauty. When this energy is active within your heart, people close to you begin to express beauty and become beautiful physically, emotionally, mentally, and spiritually.

Every Initiate of the Heart calls out beauty from those who are positively oriented. He nourishes the seeds of beauty found within the Core. Every man, in his Inner Core, is a seed of Cosmic Beauty.

It is this seventh energy of the heart that creates transformation in those who come to you for help.

This energy is easily felt by children whose heart center is awake. They build and beautify their life around people who emanate this energy which creates beauty.

In a school there was a class where the students were considered impossible rascals, and every teacher used to fear and avoid that class. One day, a new teacher came. In ten minutes he won the hearts of all the students in that class because he spoke from his heart and touched their hearts. In a short time that infamous class became the most beautiful class.

Children and teen-agers hate cover-ups and hypocrisy. They become destructive and ugly as they express their disapproval of life around them, but, in essence, they have beautiful hearts. Those who have an unfolded heart can call forth the most beautiful expressions from such a heart.

These energies of the heart become active gradually. They are not always there. One must cultivate them and make them like radiant streams of energy.

Thus, these energies can increase in their potency, but it is also possible that some of these energies slowly fade away. For example, hatred and separatism fundamentally sap these energies and make the heart empty and ugly for a while. Also, fear, greed, anger, and jealousy ruin the heart.

The eighth energy of the heart is the energy of Intuition, understanding, timelessness, and straight knowledge.

Intuition is not a hunch or feeling. It is the ability to see things from the past to the future, from cause to effect, from effect to cause, in their entire complexity and instantaneously. Intuition transcends time and sees the basic essentials.

When we are stuck in our time concept, we cannot see things as they are because we see from the viewpoint of the moment in which we live. Intuition is an understanding beyond the limitation of time.

Most of our errors are the errors of time. When things are observed from the domain of Infinity, they reveal to us their true role and their true nature. This eighth energy of the heart raises our awareness into the Infinity domain. It is after operating in this domain that our standard of values goes through a process of readjustment.

The heart also registers the formation of dark clouds in space. These clouds are composed of evil thoughts, evil plans, hatred, and separatism. Being electrical in nature, they affect the lives of people everywhere. The heart registers the existence of such clouds and passes through depressions. At such moments, mysterious heart pains are felt and irregularity of the heartbeat and heart anguish are observed.

The heart also registers all those events which bring more beauty and wealth into the space, the solar system, and the human life. Such recordings manifest themselves as bliss, ecstasy, and serenity in the heart and as an outpouring energy and enthusiasm from the heart.

Motivation comes from the heart, not from the intellect. The mind is a computer, and sometimes you do not see the errors it has been making for fifty years.

The programming of the mind is done either by our emotions or by our heart. If the programming is done by a pure heart, then the motive is correct and the computer will do good work. If the programming is done by the emotions, glamor will control the machine for a long time. The pure heart programs in accordance with the Divine Purpose. Such programming is progressive, and it meets the demands of the advancing life.

The heart never lies to you because the heart carries the Flame of Life. When you are passing through crises and are under great tension, depend on your heart. Go closer to your heart and ask its opinion about the situation. You will be surprised how clear and direct the response will be. The heart will not only reveal to you the cause of your trouble but will also show you the path to take to overcome it.

The heart thinks differently than the mind. The mind is not a dependable advisor without the overshadowing of the heart. When you do anything wrong, your mind will try to justify it or tell you that other people make greater errors and yours are small; or your mind will tell you that you are absolutely right in doing wrong and will present you with many rationalizations, self-justifications, and ways of escape. But no one can deceive the heart, and the heart never deceives anyone.

You often see a dialogue going on between the heart and a man who is identified with his mind.

The heart says, "You did wrong."

"I don't think so. I did it because of...."

"I do not know 'because.' The only thing I know is that you did wrong!"

Those who ignore their heart eventually lead it into silence. The silenced heart eventually dries up. As soon as the heart dries up, a great opportunity opens for the mind and emotions to pursue their illusions and glamors and devastate the life of the man and the lives of those with whom the man is associated.

The heart must give the command, and the intellect, like a servant, must follow it. The intellect must do the programming, but the command must come from the heart. When the motive belongs to the mind, be careful; it will be related mostly to self-interest, to separatism, to matter, to the world, and to the ego. The motive of the heart is inclusive and related to Beauty, Goodness, and Truth.

Have faith in the motives of the heart; then let your mind carry out the work in the best way possible. But do not let the mind act without the watchful eye of the heart.

Happiness and joy come to those who follow their heart. They do not have conflict in their lives. Conflict starts within you when you work against your heart. The most interesting point in human psychology is that you cannot fool the heart. The heart never agrees when you are wrong, but the mind does.

Those who follow their heart may temporarily fail from the viewpoint of the personality. Such a failure does not bring sorrow and suffering but inspires courage, leads them into greater striving, and makes them able to make greater decisions. It is not because of the heart that man fails but because of the wrong programming of the mind. The heart says, "Do not worry; we will do it again. The mind will learn from its mistakes."

The greatest healing process in the future will be the healing of the hearts of people. The heart needs healing. Because of the pressure our society is living under due to the control of illusions and glamors, the heart is left without nourishment and encouragement and thus becomes petrified, and the flame in it almost passes away. With the degeneration of the heart, the flame is not capable of sustaining the vitality of the bodies and aura, and thus various germs and sicknesses devastate the human body.

When the heart is healed and the flame is restored, the flame of the heart will open a new era of health, joy, and great endurance. The healing of the body must start with the healing of the heart. The heart must be purified; the flame must be restored.

Once this is accomplished, the healing process will take place.

No one can really heal a sick person permanently if his heart is spiritually dead or polluted by vices. Spiritually dead hearts are very dangerous. They not only contaminate people with destructive emanations, but they become graves for the incarnating human soul for many centuries. To heal a sick heart, you must bring into it love, inclusiveness, purity, joy, courage, the spirit of sacrifice, and forgiveness. These create miraculous changes in the bodies of sick people. Heal the heart and the man will be healed.

This is the age in which the heart must be put on the throne. In all human endeavors we must try to bring the influence of the heart into our daily relationships and daily labor. If there is heart in a family, that family is blessed. If there is intellect but no heart, that family will not stay together.

A scientist who is a top man in computers came to see me. First he spoke about how miraculous computers are, and he explained things which evoked my admiration. After he talked about the machines for a while, he said, "I came for counseling. I am married and have three children, but we are very unhappy. My wife and I cannot get along. I don't know what to do."

"Did you ask your heart?" I asked him.

"What?"

"Did you ask your heart?"

"What heart?"

"Your heart."

"Are you serious?"

"Yes I am. Did you ask your heart?"

"Well, I need a reasonable analysis of my situation."

"Can your computer do it?"

"What are you saying?"

"I am saying that you must try to approach your heart and see if your heart has something to tell you."

"I need your advice."

"I am not joking. I am giving you the best advice. You think your wife is wrong, don't you?"

"Yes."

"Well, ask your heart if that is true."

He got up, turned his back to me, and a few minutes later he turned and looked into my eyes with a strange smile and said, "You know, my heart says I am wrong. I knew about it long ago."

"Why didn't you listen to your heart?"

"I thought it was a sign of weakness."

"Really?"

"But great courage is needed to admit the revelation of the heart."

"Well, now you know what to do. Follow your heart and obey it. Do not escape. Do not create new programming. Follow your heart, and you will know what to do."

Our problems can only be solved through our heart; the rest is just the labor to carry the solution into life. Our university or college degrees will not help us if we do not have a healthy heart. Our certificates have no power to solve our problems; it is only our heart that solves the problems.

A wife, a husband, a child, a friend, can be understood only through the heart. The same is true in international affairs. People will never understand each other by treaties or meetings if their heart is absent. Only the heart will bring a solution to our international problems — not intellect, not diplomacy, not politics, not even power, but only the heart.

The heart forgives, but as it forgives, it becomes more watchful of the future actions of the one who was the adversary. If the mind forgives, it forgets and gives the adversary another chance to continue his destructive work. When the heart strikes, the destruction of the enemy is final because all courage and energy stream forth from the heart. The heart destroys hindrances and paves the way for the regeneration of righteousness.

We are told that Christ knows in His heart what people think. A pure heart, like radar, catches the impressions coming from a great distance. A man of pure heart has holistic perception.

The mind without a pure heart does not understand the true meanings of events. All its actions are based on self-interest, and to support its interests it rationalizes and creates excuses. The mind reads the form side of events and translates its readings for the benefit of the form. The heart reads the events as symbols. It sees the causes behind them, the relationships behind them, and it telegraphs the message of the events. For the mind, things are forms; but for the heart, things are symbols, words, sentences, and messages related to the world of causes and consciousness. The heart reads the symbology of events.

When the heart is not unfolded, the mind takes over and misleads the man, nourishing his sense of separatism. We are told that illusions are based on separatism.

The mind can be a real obstacle on the path of an unfolding and progressing heart. The heart immediately senses the truth, the fact, the reality. The mind takes that impression and translates it into the terms of personality interests; the mind tries to distort the impression and mislead the heart if the impression is not in line with self-interest. Thus the mind blinds the man; the heart awakens him. The heart goes beyond reasoning, logic, and rationalization. It goes and touches the Essence.

The heart does not justify the actions of the personality if they are not in line with Beauty, Goodness, and Truth. But the mind tries to justify actions if they bring self-interest. The heart knows immediately, but this knowledge is often clouded by mental modifications. If one catches the first flash of heart knowledge and follows it, he will never regret it. People fool themselves if they depend on their logic without using the Intuition of the heart.

The heart has direction. The heart knows the right direction. The heart is the pole star. The mind sails on, depending on the winds of self-interest.

The heart knows essentially who you are. The mind tries to cover-up. The heart knows when you are doing something wrong, but the mind tries to cover it if it is advantageous for your personality.

Most of the time a man is on the horse of his emotions and thoughts. They carry him away toward whatever direction they are urged and create a nice circus with clowns and music. But among all this noise you may have one moment of sanity, a moment of Intuition, or a moment of straight knowledge, and you see what the mind is doing in your life: wasting your energy, time, and opportunity. You see how your Self is identified with the personalities of the circus, and often with the audience itself. It is in this identification that the Self is lost, but if you want to see the Self, It is in the heart like a flame of light under all conditions.

The awakening of the man takes place when he sees himself at the moment of his identifications. The heart is the watchful eye that one cannot deceive.

When the mind develops and overrules the heart, we can expect destruction and disaster in our social, economic, and political fields. When the heart is retarded, crime increases. When the heart is empty, depression sets in.

The heart sees things on the plane of causation before they take manifestation. The mind sees the results.

The ninth energy of the heart, the recording energy, is the basic energy of telepathy. Telepathy is heart-to-heart communication, although this communication may be translated by the mind to be available to certain kinds of people.

The communication of hearts is more real than the communication of minds. The mind is related to transient things. The heart is related to the essence, to transcendental realities.

The mind deals in terms of self-interest. The heart deals in terms of wholeness.

The tenth energy of the heart is the energy which enables you to receive great inspirations and become creative. True creativity is the ability to create heroes, to create Initiates, to give birth to your divine nature.

When this tenth energy is released and begins to inspire you with higher ideas, visions, beauty, and concepts, your life becomes heroic. True heroism is nothing else but the revelation of the Divine within you through creativity. The objectification of Cosmic inspiration produces heroes.

All creative energies pour from the heart. Intuition, love, striving, and sacrifice are the streams of the heart. They nourish. They harmonize. They reveal and synthesize. All that the heart creates is based on Beauty, Goodness, and Truth.

The heart transforms a person. The heart creates a new man out of the old. The heart can create a new race, a new society, a new life.

The mind creates laws, but crimes increase. The heart creates a sense of responsibility, the spirit of respect, love, and righteousness, and the laws become obsolete. It is the heart that has the essence of laws. The mind forces the laws. The heart transforms the man through love.

Beauty streams out of the heart. Those who have unfolded hearts are sources of beauty. Beauty is not an intellectual quality but a heart quality.

The heart is for the future. The intellect is for the present or for the past. Those who have a pure heart see the future, sense the future, and work for the future. Without the heart, the intellect works at digging in the past or utilizing knowledge for temporary pleasures.

The eleventh energy of the heart operates as the transmuting fire. The transmutation of physical, emotional, mental, global, and universal forces and energies takes place in our heart.

In the constitution of man we have four lower etheric planes, the totality of which is our etheric body, the electromagnetic body around and in the physical form. We also have, beyond our mental plane, four very fiery planes which are called Cosmic Ethers. As the human evolution proceeds, the higher ethers gradually replace the lower ethers. This replacement process is carried out through transmutation. This transmutation takes place in the fire of the heart.

As the transmutation is carried out, man enters into "divinehood." Man enters into his divine heritage and slowly becomes aware of the life and mysteries going on upon all higher Cosmic Ethers. In other words, man is now equipped with more subtle and divine mechanisms through which he can see millions of years ahead and wield power through great wisdom and in accordance with the Purpose of the Great Life. He becomes a Master because he masters his individual world and gains power to master greater worlds. Then the higher ethers replace the lower ethers, and he, in his physical brain consciousness, becomes a divine embodiment because now he achieves continuity of consciousness in the higher planes and in the Higher Worlds.

This transmutation and transformation is carried out in the heart, and the result is Transfiguration, Renunciation, and eventually Revelation.

Initiations are taken according to the ratio of the higher ethers replacing the lower ethers. As this transmutation process goes on, we see another phenomenon happening in the form of the human being: each of his seven vehicles simultaneously goes through a process of "purification," as for example, a pure spring purifies the old muddy waters of a lake. Similarly, the highest substance of each plane, which is called the atomic plane, pours down through the levels and replaces them. Thus, as the etheric transmutation goes on, the other planes also go through a process of transmutation, transformation, and transfiguration.

The heart is the synthesizer; diversity is changed into synthesis in the heart. The heart links all that exists and causes transformation in them. It acts as the sun in our being.

The heart is the abode of the Flame of Life. This flame is rooted in the Fire of Space. The Fire of Space is the source of all life, in any form. When the flame of the heart is lit, it links the person to the creative energies in Space, makes the person a source of creativity, nourishes the fires of each atom, of each cell in the bodies, and glows throughout the aura with a golden hue.

The heart protects all life-forms which are striving to express beauty and to serve the Purpose of the

Great Life. Each human heart, each heart in any living form is a dispenser of life, is a transmitter of life. It is only through the heart that the life thread is found and conscious immortality is reached.

We are told that an Arhat is a Flame of Life, and "He sees through the eyes of the heart." An Arhat is a person Who has made a total commitment to Beauty, Goodness, and Truth; a total commitment to Life. A total commitment is a total renouncement of selfhood.

The weakest person in the world is the one who has no commitment. The best husband is a husband who has a commitment to his wife. The best wife is a wife who has a real commitment to her husband. If one has no commitment, he is a parasite. A parasite lives off the lives of others. Manhood and womanhood start from the moment of commitment. A commitment is the decision that you are going to dedicate yourself to the highest good and meet your promises and your visions with your utmost dedication.

Your knowledge, the storage of your information, does not increase your value if you do not have a commitment to great values because a commitment is the moment in which your knowingness changes into beingness; it is the moment of your transformation. You can contact reality only during the moment of your commitment. People who have a real commitment to great values are the people who form the foundations of the new race.

The Ancients used to say that the heart is the most mysterious temple because God dwells in it.

There are two kinds of people: those who live for the flame of the heart, and those who live for matter, for their self-interest. Those who live for the flame of the heart are those who spread joy, who transform people, who manifest beauty, who protect life, and who inspire courage, striving, and labor.

The twelfth energy of the heart creates the power of righteousness and compassion. When this energy is active, every kind of unrighteousness disappears from your life and compassion fills your heart because this energy puts you in harmony with the Cosmic rhythm. All that you do becomes an effort to synchronize yourself with the symphony of the Cosmos. Your life becomes a symphony instead of becoming the noise of "rock and roll."

Compassion is a great healing power. The great artist Nicholas Roerich has a painting in which we see beautiful high mountains, a blue and purple sky, and on the right on the rocks, a hermit. If we visualize the painting in motion, we see a hunter releasing an arrow at a running deer. The deer is seeking refuge with the hermit. The hermit, with deep love for the deer, is extending his right hand to protect the deer from the flying arrow. The arrow is piercing his hand, but his hand is saving the beautiful deer. The painting is called "Compassion." Compassion is the power that heals.

It is possible to train the heart, to unfold the etheric heart center, and to make it a fountain of bliss. The _first_ step to train the heart is to exercise love and compassion. Compassion is the ability to see your oneness with all that exists. This must start from childhood and be carried out throughout life. Children must be taught how to be compassionate and to respect life in all its forms.

It is also possible to cultivate compassion through meditation to open one's heart center. The following meditation is a very beautiful tool to cultivate compassion:

1. Sit comfortably and relax.

2. Close your eyes.

3. Take a few deep breaths and relax further.

4. Visualize the following:

   — Birds singing on a beautiful blooming tree

   — Fish of various colors playing in a pool

   — Flowers of many colors in the fields

   — Various animals feeding their babies

   — Children playing in the fields

   — Pine forests

   — Stars in the midnight sky

5. Take each one for a month and touch them, love them, admire the joy of life in them. Then think that all of these living beings want to enjoy life, want to bring joy and

beauty to others. Feel their heartbeats, their desire to live, to be, to enjoy.

6. Think about nations and wish every nation greater joy and success. Bless each of them and send your love and peace to them.

7. Think about one humanity and see humanity as one family. Feel the desire of humanity to liberate itself, to free itself from wars, pains, and sufferings and enjoy life in peace, in love, and in understanding.

8. See all boundaries eliminated and nations fused with each other, forming one global brotherhood.

9. Visualize our solar system as a spaceship with twelve wheels in the great ocean of the Milky Way. See how it is necessary to be in harmony with the great Center of Love and Compassion beyond the galaxy.

10. See the Central Sun from Whom emanates everything, and to Whom returns every Spark of Life.

11. Decide to increase your love.

12. Decide to be compassionate to all living forms.

13. Feel your heart filling with joy and bliss.

14. Sing a song of gratitude to the All-pervading Life.

15. Open your eyes, sit quietly for a few moments, and then go about your work.

The _second_ step to train the heart is to exercise generosity and to increase your generosity. Learn to give. Every week give something useful to somebody. At the end of the year give many things, but give with joy.

Givers are called the companions of God. All Great Ones are givers. They give in generosity because the ultimate success is to lose their cards in the game of life.

The _third_ step to train the heart is to learn to develop serenity and to keep calm in trying conditions. Identification with spiritual values naturally brings you into great serenity.

Any irritation in your nervous system reflects in the heart and damages its fiery petals. Any irritation burns parts of your nadis and blackens parts of your aura. Serenity creates the condition in which the flower of your heart blooms.

The _fourth_ step to train the heart is to develop the capacity to think clearly and have pure thoughts. Ugly, harmful, and separative thoughts damage the heart and disturb its rhythm. They change the chemistry of the blood and glandular secretions. Pure thoughts are thoughts based on Beauty, Goodness, Truth, Simplicity, and Nobility.

The _fifth_ step to train the heart is to resign from any ugly, harmful, or selfish actions, words, or expressions. The heart is a sensitive electrical web. Every act, word, or expression that is not in harmony with the symphony of life creates disturbances in the electrical field of the web. Thoughts based on fear, hatred, anger, greed, and jealousy burn the petals of the heart. Joy, beauty, freedom, and compassion nourish the heart.

The heart loves wisdom, so try to feed the heart with wisdom. Wisdom is the ability to see things from objective and subjective viewpoints, from past and future viewpoints, from individual and collective viewpoints. The flame of the heart distills the past experiences, the accumulated knowledge of lives, and produces wisdom.

The *sixth* step is optimism. Optimism gives vitality to the heart. Try to see the birth side of events. Develop hope and think about a victorious future. Know that yours is the victory, yours is the future, because no one can prevent your success and progress once you dedicate yourself to Beauty, Goodness, and Truth. The heart in the Sacred Teaching is called "the Abode of God."[3]

The *seventh* step is to develop altruism. Altruism is a benevolent activity, a life lived in generosity, selflessness, and philanthropy.

Through altruism a person becomes a radiant light. He not only becomes philanthropic in the physical field but also in the mental, moral, and spiritual fields. He becomes a lover of humanity, a

---

3. Agni Yoga Society, *Heart*, para. 73.

lover of life. He falls in love with living forms and opens himself to life.

This is a very blissful state of the soul in which he feels one with life. All Great Saviors demonstrated altruism, and it made Their hearts turn into rivers of Life.

The *eighth* step is to cultivate the following virtues:

- group love

- humility

- service

- patience

- joy

- tolerance (Intuition)

- synthesis (heart and head)

- compassion

- sympathy (to tune in your frequency with other frequencies)

- wisdom

- sacrifice

- gratitude

The *ninth* step is to live in areas that have pure air, the beauty of Nature, and serenity.

People talk about their heart as if it were their property. In the Sacred Teaching of Agni Yoga we are told that the heart does not belong to us; it is given from Above. It is called "an international organ," "a vessel of universal energy."

It is in the heart that the rays of all principles meet. It is in the heart that Cosmos reflects Itself. One can imagine all hearts as being the flowers of a garland through which flows the Cosmic Life.

People are sometimes used to saying, "Did someone steal your heart?" This is not a poetic expression but an expression of fact. Our heart can be vacated and only the earthly frame can remain, which then serves as a dwelling for dark forces. Such people are called heartless people who exploit their fellow beings, destroy the life-giving elements of Nature, organize global crimes, and try to lead humanity to the worship of matter, money, and sex.

There are many things to avoid which hurt one's heart, for example: meat, alcohol, hallucinogenic drugs, large doses of aspirin, heavy medications, *imperil,* caffeine, celery, cabbage, excessive oil and sugar, excessive sex, sleepless nights or long hours of entertainment, noise, electrical radiation, radioactive materials, smog, various poisonous gases, rock and disco music, and other such kinds of music.

Too much talk is very harmful to the heart, as are worry and fear. These act as poisons in the heart. Hatred creates *angina pectoris*, or spasms in the artery which nourishes the heart.

The heart generates compassionate energy. If this energy is not used in philanthropic activities or

loving actions, enlargement of the heart occurs —
cor bovinum.

As one exercises compassion, the cure slowly
penetrates the heart. When the heart is active with
this energy, it rejuvenates the organism and radiates
healing energies around the man.

It is also very interesting to notice that the heart
controls the memory banks. Also, the heart has control over our consciousness. As our heart fails, our
memory fades and our consciousness weakens.

People talk about immunity. The heart contains
the secret of immunity against all poisons. A
radioactive heart rejects all causes of diseases. We
are told that in the heart there is a magnetic center
which is called the "magnet of the heart." It is this
magnet which synthesizes all fiery energies of the
Cosmos. The magnetic center, like a seed, grows and
radiates throughout millions of incarnations if we
feed it with benevolent thoughts, beauty, and goodness.

our magnet to the future

The miracle of the metamorphosis of the divine
seed, called the human soul, takes place in the sacred
chamber of the Chalice.

There are two Chalices in man. One is called the
twelve-petaled Lotus, located in the Higher Mind.
The other chalice is formed by the spleen, the solar
plexus, and the heart chakras. This is also called the
chalice, the lower chalice.

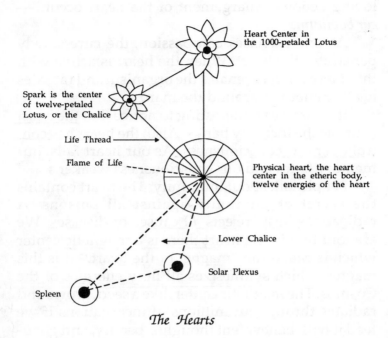

The Hearts

The life thread emanates from the center of the twelve-petaled Lotus and anchors itself in the heart. All physical, emotional, and mental *transmutations* take place in the sanctuary of the heart through the fire of the Flame of Life. It is through this Flame that the process called transmutation, transformation, and transfiguration takes place on the physical, the physical-astral, and the physical-mental planes up to the Third Initiation. During the Third Initiation, the Initiate passes through the fire of the heart and travels toward the twelve-petaled Lotus, via the heart center in the head.

Once he passes through the fire of the heart, the spleen, or its etheric counterpart, is used as a station to receive impressions from the physical plane. The solar plexus is used to receive impressions from the astral world. The heart center in the head is used to receive impressions from the mental plane. These three centers synthesize the senses of their planes.

The passage through the fire of the heart is possible only if the human soul demonstrates in his many incarnations self-forgetfulness, harmlessness, sacrificial service, labor, and deep compassion.

As the disciple accumulates enough merit, he is led to the gate of the heart. In the sacred chamber of the Chalice, the One Initiator watches silently the process of the metamorphosis of the human being. When the man awakens into his Divinity and, for the first time in his long journey, sees the face of the One Who stands at the gate of the Cosmic Mystery, he receives His fire. Now man is a newborn soul, and his light radiates throughout the three worlds.

All the dross of the ages in all three lower planes is burned in the fire of the heart. His body is pure, his emotional body shines like a mirror, and his mental body reflects the mysteries of creative forces.

Healing is accomplished. It is only after the Transfiguration that man demonstrates shining health in his three vehicles and his presence radiates healing power.

We are told that after one passes through the flame of the heart, he becomes a transmitter of life energy. He brings life to all his contacts through his eyes, touch, words, and silent thoughts. He transmits the purifying fire. He transmits the fire of creativity and love and joy. He transmits the fire of bliss and enthusiasm. Enthusiasm is a process of "burning" by the fire of Divine Purpose.

It is after this fiery Initiation that one becomes a healer. His healing power and wisdom increase as he travels toward the unfolding Chalice, and eventually he passes through the Flame in the Chalice and becomes an immortal being.

This is how the progress of the human soul becomes a pilgrimage on the path of fire through the gates of flames.

The heart echoes "...the Highest Guidance."[4]

---

4. Agni Yoga Society, *Heart*, para. 69.

❦ The Twelve Virtues of the Heart

There are twelve virtues of the heart. Each virtue is a petal of flame in the heart center.

The first virtue may be called **group love, group consciousness, or cooperation in group formation.**

When the first flame of the heart center begins to unfold, you develop

- selflessness

- harmlessness

- right speech

- sense of responsibility

- intuitive perception of the need

- a power of subordination of your opinions, desires, and interests to the immediate need of the group

The group can be your family, your immediate friends, your church, your nation, or humanity.

When a person develops this virtue of the heart, he begins to live for the benefit of others. He fills their physical, emotional, and mental needs "through self-forgetfulness, harmlessness, and right speech."

If this virtue does not manifest, then you use everything that you have and everything that you are for your selfish interests at the expense of others.' This is how people become evil.

Harmfulness is a state of consciousness in which you utilize all your resources and the resources of others for your self-interest. This first virtue cures you from such a disease.

When you have group love, you no longer deceive people. You develop a pure heart and a pure spirit. Group love makes you feel that you are one with the group. Group love develops the sense of responsibility within you. You never think, speak, or act in a way that hinders the progress, success, or development of the group members.

The sense of responsibility makes you love in such a way that through your thoughts, words, and deeds you help people improve their lives.

Group love helps you increase your intuitive perception. Intuition never develops in people who are contaminated by jealousy, revenge, and materialism. This is why they eventually defeat themselves when they can no longer solve their increasing problems through their mental powers. Intuitive people are future victors.

Group love holds people together in cooperation. Cooperation is a united labor of hearts which expands the consciousness and rejects any self-interest. Our consciousness expands first through the virtue of group love; second, through detachment; third, through renunciation; fourth, through givingness; and fifth, through the joy of labor.

Cooperation is the development of self-initiated labor in the light of Hierarchy. Co-workers have five characteristics. They are heroic, kind, noble, intelligent, and intuitive. Through these signs one can know that the first virtue is in operation.

The second virtue of the heart is **humility.** Humility is the awareness of your exact place on the ladder of perfection. People think they are either at the top or the bottom of the ladder. Such people have no awareness of where they are. How can you live a conscious life if you are not aware of your exact place on the ladder of evolution?

When you know your location, you look up and see millions of people ahead of you; you look back and see millions of people behind you. You feel responsible for those behind you, and you feel adoration for those who are ahead of you. This creates striving in you. Humility grows with the sense of responsibility and with the spirit of striving.

Humility saves you from vanity and pride. Once a girl stood in front of a mirror and started shouting to her mother, "Mother, I am the most beautiful girl in the world."

"No, honey," said her mother. "There are also other beautiful girls in the world."

"But not as pretty as I am…."

This is an example of vanity. Sometimes our vanities lead us into the most dangerous traps. A humble person knows his weaknesses in spite of the flattery and praise given to him by others. He even rejects praise because in his humility he sees those who have greater abilities than he has. Thus, humility makes a person strive and never be satisfied with his achievements.

Pride and vanity lead you to artificiality. Eventually you become a machine in the hands of others if you live in your vanities.

When you feel vain and prideful, remember your failures and look at those who are far ahead of you. Humility makes you measure the space which you can occupy.

Someone once told me, "In my next incarnation I will be the teacher of all the South American countries."

I replied, "Too much space…."

A little bird must know how much space he can cross with his little wings.

The inability to recognize your *resources* and your *capabilities* leads you into vanity. You must not imagine that you can act as an elephant if you are an ant. You must see how much needs to be achieved and conquered if you want to keep your humility in the moments of your success.

3) The third virtue of the heart is **service.** Actions, emotions, thoughts, or plans based upon or originated from Beauty, Goodness, Righteousness,

Joy, Freedom, and Truth are called service. Service is used to uplift, to heal, to lead, to direct people toward higher understanding, to expand their consciousness, and to lead them into sacrificial living.

Service is the radiation of the light of the soul which purifies, gives joy, enlightens, and creates striving. Striving is an inner effort to make your life better and more useful.

 The fourth virtue of the heart is **patience.** Patience is a state of consciousness in which you are aware that you are an endless, infinite, and immortal being. When you have such an inner awareness in any event or condition in your life or in the world, you are a patient human being because you observe the situation or condition in the light of endlessness, infinity, and immortality. In patience you do not lose any time; you do not lose any opportunity; but you know that things follow the natural laws and that you cannot make a seed grow and be a tree in one day.

Patience is always inspired by hope and by the future. Patience is a special wisdom which realizes that in time all will be possible. With patience we gather great amounts of experience and adjust ourselves to the demands of the future.

 The next virtue of the heart is **labor.** Through labor man feels the urge to give himself a new birth. Through labor his hidden talents and beauty are brought out into the world in creative activities. Energy evoked by labor makes man work in harmony with the Plan of the Hierarchy, in the right place, at the right time, and for the right duration.

Labor is carried out in the light of your spiritual and earthly tasks. Labor is the ability to cooperate with the creative forces in Nature to carry into manifestation the Divine Will.

6) The sixth virtue of the heart is **tolerance.** Real tolerance is achieved when one steps beyond his mental reasoning and logic and functions in the awareness of the Intuitional Plane. A person will be fanatical to a certain degree until he focuses his consciousness in the Intuitional Plane. The mind always separates and thinks in duality. The Intuition *thinks* in terms of wholeness and synthesis.

In tolerance, your vision is 360 degrees wide and above the surface of the earth. Tolerance is the ability to see the relationship between everything that exists and your independence from any limitation.

Fanaticism first manifests as silent condemnation of everything that exists. Then it turns into violence and crime. Tolerance is the ability to understand others and give them a chance to grow. In tolerance, one respects the freedom of people as long as they do not impose themselves on others.

People sometimes think that you must tolerate other people's crimes, violence, and ugliness. This is not tolerance. Tolerance is not passivity. Tolerance leaves you free to exercise your creative powers to progress and achieve, to grow and bloom. But tolerance turns into a sword if you prevent people from being beautiful, free, creative, and successful.

My father used to say that tolerance is a double edged sword. One edge is love, respect, and understanding; the other edge is balance, fortitude, sternness, and lightning. If one misunderstands tolerance, he turns into a football on the field of self-seeking people.

A fanatical person is one who generally sticks to the past or to self-interest. He may also be stuck with contemporary values, but he seldom thinks about future values and the interests of other people. A tolerant person is not stuck with the past and the present. He strives for future achievements.

The seventh virtue of the heart is **spiritual identification.** Spiritual identification is the ability to fuse your consciousness with the physical, emotional, mental, and spiritual states of others but still remain a detached observer. In this way, you understand and know exactly what people are. In advanced degrees of spiritual identification, you can even identify with animals and trees and know them exactly as they are.

This virtue leads you to feel that you are one with the whole Universe. Through spiritual identification, you can even share the pains and sufferings of others in order to release them from their pressures and tensions. This is often called "experiencing sacred pains."

Through spiritual identification, you can also draw a great amount of knowledge and wisdom. Great service can be rendered to others by having firsthand knowledge about them through the virtue of spiritual identification. Spiritual identification leads into universality and synthesis. Through identification you become free from the habit of criticism because you see your oneness with others.

8)   **Compassion** is the eighth virtue of the heart. It is the ability to see all conflicting forces and the reasons for their conflict. It is the ability to see the contributions of conflicting forces. Compassion is a state of beingness of one who is in close contact with the Heart of Cosmos. Compassion is inclusive love and understanding.

Compassion is the ability to be one with the Self in every living form in Nature. It is the ability to see that all is emanated from the One Self.

9)   **Sympathy** is the ninth virtue of the heart. It is the basis of physical, emotional, mental, and spiritual cooperation and harmony, not with the personality aspect of another but with the striving Self in the person. Through sympathy we can see what other people are, exactly the way their Self is watching them. We are told that when the knowledge petals of the Chalice open, sympathy increases in our heart. Remember that the petals of the Chalice and the petals of the heart are different devices of radiation.

10)   **Wisdom** is the tenth virtue of the heart. Through wisdom man achieves the ability to use the treasury of all the experiences of his past. He develops Intuition to see the future results and effects of every action and thought. He sees exactly the need of the moment. He gains stability and equilibrium in trying conditions.

Intuition is like a sudden revelation in which you see all that is to be seen. Wisdom is the power of application of the revelation in such a way that the revelation can be brought to life and can create constructive results. To do this you need experience, intelligence, compassion, a creative mind, and a virtuous life. All these are summed up in wisdom.

The eleventh virtue of the heart is called **sacrifice.** Sacrifice is will, bliss, and fiery energies which transmute, transform, and transfigure people. Sacrifice makes a person realize the values of spiritual realities and, in the light of the future glory, he gives all that is necessary to achieve that glory. This energy has the power to sanctify and make holy all those with whom you come in contact. It is through sacrifice that things really progress in the world. It is through sacrifice that greater contacts are built between you and the Subtle Worlds. It is through sacrifice that the inner beauty comes forth.

The greatest measure of a leader is the measure of his sacrifice. We are measured by that which we sacrifice and give. Our greatness is built by the power of renunciation and sacrifice.

The twelfth virtue of the heart is **gratitude.** Gratitude is the ability to appreciate all the labor done in the Universe by the Creative Forces. It is the ability to accept the beauty and the glory of existence.

I remember bathing in a hot springs under the stars. Everything was so beautiful that I talked to God and said, "Lord, how pleasant, beautiful, and joyful is everything. You created all of this. How grateful I am to You." Tears came from my eyes, and I felt the preciousness of life.

Gratitude is the ability to appreciate the gifts of life given to you — the air, the sky, the ocean, beautiful people, your consciousness, your future…. Gratitude is appreciation of the various kinds of help on various levels which you receive from life. Gratitude is appreciation for the forces which work for you, which protect you, and which give you the opportunity to transcend your level of beingness.

These are the twelve petals of the heart.

Blessed are those who make their heart bloom. Only such hearts will have conscious communication with the Heart of Cosmos and proceed consciously toward that Heart.

4

🍂 *Mind and Heart*

People sometimes wonder whether the heart or the mind is the most important factor in life, and which one must be developed most to guarantee success and progress.

In general, there are three kinds of people. The first kind are those who are dedicated to the development of their mind. The second kind are those who are dedicated to developing their heart. The third kind are those who try to develop their heart and mind simultaneously. This third kind are not the majority, but they hold the key to equilibrium in their hands.

The first are dedicated only to the development of their mind because they think that the mind brings success, prosperity, victory, etc. They develop their mind through academic studies and college education. They become scientists, physicians, lawyers, businessmen, etc. They develop their lower mind to such a degree that their heart remains far behind.

When the mind is developed and the heart is ignored, the following things happen:

1. A person develops separatism. He may be a politician, educator, philosopher, communicator, scientist, artist, or even a theologian or financier. But in all these fields, he develops a deep sense of separatism.

The mind divides. The mind thinks in terms of "mine and yours." Separatism eventually builds a wall in the mind, and the person is left with the lower side of his nature and deprived of his higher, divine nature. Such a person gradually becomes destructive because he always tries to hurt the interests of other people. This is the cause of revolutions, conflicts, and wars.

2. If the mind is cultivated without the heart, the person develops an ego. He begins to think that he is the only valuable person in the world. He looks at others as inferior beings who have no right even to live or exist. He thinks that his certificates, knowledge, position, and possessions are the only things that make him a valuable person. His ego slowly turns into his curse, and life becomes for him either boring or a never-ending path of pleasures to make him forget about his misery.

An ego always tends to manipulate others. An ego can make the righteous person seem to be a criminal, and the criminal a righteous person. He can quickly make people guilty or innocent according to his own egotistical interests.

The more one develops his ego, the less he exists as a human being. People become non-existent through developing their egos. The Real Self slowly disappears, and an artificial person comes into being: a person built by the trash of physical, emotional, and mental illusions and glamors.

Egotism is an advanced sickness. It is a cancer-like growth in the aura of man, and it is very difficult to be healed from it. You can see egos sitting at home, in offices, and in public positions. They are all mind, knowledge, and information; but separative and self-seeking. Those who develop their ego eventually discover that the cause of all their miseries is their ego. And because they cannot resign from their ego, they try to *love to suffer* rather than give up their ego.

3. If the mind is cultivated without the heart, the person develops an urge to dominate, rule, and force his will. The development of the mind gives one the sense of power and an urge to control the lives of other people and bring them under his will. Dictators and totalitarians are created on this path.

Dictators are found not only in the political field but also in all walks of life. Even in religion they are well known. Such people have big egos. They are separative and aggressive. They are totalitarian because, due to their mental development, they feel they have the right to rule the lives of other human beings, generally for their own interest.

Power is always self-destructive unless it is balanced by reason and the heart. Power manipulates, prevents the development of others, and creates in others an intense resistance, especially when it is used for self-interest or separative group interest. Power spreads like a cancer and dominates others by all ways and means so that it can increase itself. But as a person increases in power, he becomes empty of his True Self. When the Self withdraws, it is replaced by destruction. Power makes a person its own slave.

One can be free while being a slave of another human being. But if one is his own slave, there is no hope for him to have true freedom. This is why the Ancients used to say that power blinds people, and a blind leader is the most dangerous leader.

4. If the mind is cultivated without the heart, the person develops the desire to possess without limit; the desire to possess people, objects, and properties. This can often be seen in families with several children. The most mentally developed child tries to possess the others, to use them for his own interests and the accumulation of wealth as he grows.

The urge to possess and accumulate possessions is a real psychological sickness, as dangerous as any serious physical sickness. To satisfy his desires, the person with such an urge begins to commit legal or illegal crimes. As the mind progresses without the heart, the person's crimes increase because the developed mind gives the person the feeling that he can do anything he wants and save himself from any trap.

When the heart is dead, the person develops greed; nothing satisfies him. He must possess more and more to feel secure. When he feels insecure, he develops a deep-seated fear. This makes the situation worse.

It is very interesting to notice that the most obedient servants of intellectuals are those who developed their mind without developing their heart. These intellectuals encourage people by every means to develop their mind so that they can be useful for the intellectual's own plans. An awakened heart cannot be enslaved or bribed. A person becomes enslaved by other people through his own mind. The mind can be enslaved, but not the heart.

You can make the body of a person your slave if his mind is developed, but you cannot control his heart. It is the heart that leads people toward freedom, not the mind. The heart is the foundation of a freedom which can be carried to completion by developing the mind to a similar degree.

A mentally developed person is the symbol of greed if he has no heart. He wants to possess and possess. He never feels satisfied. Possessiveness is a sign that there is a vacuum in the person, a sign that the heart is not there. When the chest is empty of a heart, the person feels urged to fill that vacuum with his possessions. And the possessions are acquired by the power of separatism, egotism, manipulation, and greed.

Greed is like a bucket whose bottom has fallen out. Nothing can fill it. Exploitation carried out through the subtleties of the mind gradually takes away your flesh and leaves you only with your bones. You do not realize that you have been led to the abyss of your destruction.

5. When the mind is cultivated without the heart, the person develops vanity. Vanity is identification with the form of the exaggerated imagination you have about yourself. You imagine that you are something that you are not. You identify with that image and live as that image.

Vanity belittles and insults others and denies their value and their rights. The false image built by vanity gradually replaces the real person. When the replacement is complete, the whole mechanism of the person functions under an unreal image. This is a great disaster for the future of the person because the harder he tries to find his True Self, the deeper he goes into his false self. This is how man runs after his shadow, thinking that he is his shadow.

Mental development without the heart leads man toward mirages. When the heart is developed with the mind, it continuously reminds the person about his real identity.

6. Those who cultivate their mind without their heart develop materialism. For such people all is matter, and beyond their knowledge and experience, nothing exists. They cannot explain how they think, how creative geniuses come into being, how the senses of beauty, logic, reasoning, love, and compassion are created. All is matter for them.

For a materialist there is no soul; there is no immortality. For a materialist the Supreme Mind does not exist — all is matter. One wonders how to explain the existence of the Cosmic Laws to such a person!

When the mind is developed without the heart, it severs its connection with the Higher Worlds. The lower mind enslaves such people, and they run in the labyrinth of their concrete mind which deals only with matter. Usually such people develop intense cruelty and violence in order to reach their goals, as other people seem to them like material objects.

When the mind is developed at the expense of the heart, the heart no longer transmits the feeling of humanness, love, and compassion, and the mind ruthlessly attacks its victims.

7. When the mind is cultivated without the heart, the person develops an advanced technique of exploitation. Exploitation has its chain-links: it starts with separatism, egotism, dictatorship, possession, vanity, materialism, and ends with exploitation.

Exploitation is heartless action. A person who exploits employs any means to use other people for his own advantage. He tries to prevent people from educating their heart and from achieving higher positions so that he can exploit them. Exploitation is evident in all departments of human endeavor, but those who exploit lose their joy and eventually fall into despair.

What happens if you develop your heart and ignore your mind? This is as bad as the development of the mind without the heart. Such people think that all miseries and the increasing dangers of final annihilation are developed by those who have well-cultivated minds, who know all the ways and means to lead humanity to pollution, to economic disaster, and to a final war. So, they turn their faces toward the development of the heart.

The heart is developed through intense devotion, worship, love, compassion, suffering, and pain. But if the mind is not developed, all these fine qualities lead one to self-defeat.

When the heart is developed without the mind, the following things happen:

1.   The person loses his identity, his self-esteem, and his self-image. He becomes all-giving, without discernment and discrimination. Such people forget that as individuals they are sacred; they have great individual value and rights. We cannot really serve others if we are a nobody. The sense of individuality is the foundation by which we reach others and help them.

It is possible that one can consciously sacrifice his individual interests to the common interest. This is a great virtue. But one must have *himself* before he is able to give himself to others. People say that they have given everything to gain the kingdom of God, but what did they give? In most cases, their behavior is a covered escape from duties and responsibilities and a way to be a burden on the shoulders of others.

People think that giving is good, but it is a very dangerous act:

    a. if you do not have discrimination

    b. if through your giving you are encouraging weakness and crime

    c. if you are making yourself a headache for others or making yourself dependent; or if you are developing pride in yourself that you can give and you can sacrifice

Such people give up all that they have but impose greatly on society to help them continue their "selfless" lives.

2. Those who develop their heart without their mind become all-loving or goody-goody. Loving without the use of your mind turns into a source of unending problems. People forget that love is not an emotion but a light, when it is kindled by the mind. Love is not an act of surrendering yourself to a criminal; it is the ability to control him and transform him.

Love is not an act of surrendering yourself to those who intend to destroy you. It is an act to protect your own values in order to help others to develop their values. If you feed a criminal with your love, you make him stronger. But if your love is used to transform him, you destroy the criminal in him. Blind love sometimes causes greater damage than wise indifference.

People are sometimes confused between love and pity. They think that pity is love in action. Once I asked a pregnant sixteen-year-old girl who was suffering with gonorrhea and syphilis, "Why did you sleep with that person?"

Her immediate answer was, "He looked so miserable. He needed love, and I gave it to him."

I do not think that such pity is recorded as interest in our spiritual bank account.

Love is an energy, and it must be applied intelligently. All-givingness and all-lovingness are the qualities of a superior person if they are enlightened by the light of intelligence.

Once a family was traveling on a highway when they saw a man walking under the scorching sun. The wife said, "Let's help him." The husband said, "I don't know who he is." The children said, "It is very hot for him." They stopped and took the man into their car. A few minutes later the man pulled out a revolver and forced the husband to pull over toward some bushes near a hill. He made them get out of the car, robbed the father and mother, shot them, left the children, and took off with the car.

My father used to say, "Do not pay one thousand dollars to buy some straw." A heart that is developed without the mind will always find thousands of reasons to justify the sacrifice.

3. A heart that is developed without the mind makes a person all-agreeing. He agrees with right and left because he cannot see any difference between them. Such a person can be *used* for any direction.

Once I was on an airplane. A lady sat next to me and asked if I believed in the Lord. I said, "Yes, of course." Then she continued to ask other questions until I decided to have some fun.

"You know," I said, "I don't think there is any God because of the presence of all the evil we see around us. How can evil live in God?"

She thought for a few minutes and said, "I always had a doubt about His existence, but I didn't know why."

"Now tell me why He does not exist," I asked.

She said, "Because innocent children die from grave sicknesses, war, depression...a Father can't stand that."

I thought she had gone too far, so I said, "I wonder Who is the One Who created all these stars, galaxies, and constellations...."

"Make up your mind," she said. "If you really believe He exists, then I, too, will believe in His existence."

She was a wealthy lady. A person with a developed mind and an undeveloped heart could have had a great "feast" with her.

Develop your questioning mind with your heart. Do not agree with everything. See, touch, examine, analyze, relate, and then choose your action.

I remember a grandmother who was all heart. A stranger came and said to her, "Your grandson needs one thousand dollars and a few gold rings. He is in trouble. You and I must take the money and jewelry and save him."

The grandmother became so excited that she took one thousand dollars from a hidden drawer and a few rings and said, "Let's go." They walked for ten minutes. Then the stranger said, "Do you see that building? He is upstairs in one of the rooms. We must hurry."

When they reached the entrance to the large building, the man said, "You sit and wait here until I come back with your grandson. Give me the money and rings."

"Take care…. Be careful," she said to him.

The grandmother sat waiting until dark when her grandson found her sitting at the entrance to the big building.

"What are you doing here, Grandmother?"

"I am so happy you are released. Where is the man?"

"Which man?"

"Well…." And she told the whole story and concluded with, "But he should still be in the building because he didn't come out of this entrance."

"Grandmother, the building has many doors, and you are watching only one of them. Let us go home…."

4. A person who develops his heart without his mind eventually loses all his possessions because those who develop their mind without their heart take advantage of such people. People sometimes say, "Good people are poor. Evil people are rich." This is not true. You can be rich with the qualities of your heart and mind, and you can be poor because of your stupidity and laziness. If the heart is not

supported by the mind, it cannot survive in the complicated situations of life.

If you have all heart but no mind, your partner who is all mind without heart will exploit you, take over your business, and then throw you out into the street. He will even take over your home and your belongings because he does not care about you. He is interested in what you have, not in what you are.

If you have rulers or legislators who do not have heart, eventually and perhaps unconsciously, they will lead you into poverty and slavery. The mind is always separative and possessive. It is never satisfied with what it collects; it always wants more.

5. When the heart is developed without the mind, the person slowly develops a slave psychology and becomes dominated by those who have developed their mind but not their heart. People who have greater intellectual capacity and knowledge dominate those who have less or no intellectual power.

At present, the ruler of the world is the mind, not the heart. A person who has a developed heart but no mental development cannot protect his rights and his freedom. Freedom cannot be gained by emotions and excitement but by well-made plans and goal-fitting actions. Those who fight for their freedom with their emotions make the job of ruling them easier for dictators. The heart cannot fight alone until its superior powers are awakened by cooperation with the mind.

Once a father said to his son, "If you want to be somebody and have power over multitudes, without being the slave of others, you must develop your mind."

"But I don't want to have power over others."

"Then you are going to be the slave of those who have developed their minds."

Poor man, he didn't know that he was leading his son into the worst kind of slavery.

One day a boy came to me and said, "Whatever I do ends in failure. Finally I have realized that failure and misery lead me into initiation. I am realizing that I must not make any more efforts to be successful and rich because I want to be initiated. Doesn't poverty enlighten me and cause my advancement? Isn't poverty a gift from God?"

"No, not at all," I answered. "You do not know what you are talking about. God is abundance. God is a challenge for never-ending progress and success. Do not cover-up your laziness and weakness and insult God by saying that He is leading you into initiation through misery and poverty."

"But didn't Christ say that we must renounce everything?"

"Yes, He said that, but what can you renounce when you have nothing?"

Intellectual coyotes enjoy such fools, using them as desserts for their dinners. What a sacrilegious act it is to blame God for our miseries and failures.

6. Those who develop their heart without their mind become visionaries. To have a vision is good, but vision must be actualized through the mind. You see people sitting and imagining that things will be better in the future. Things will not be better

in the future if you do not *make* things better in the future.

Vision can grow and expand to such a degree that, like a balloon, it pulls you up and you lose your ground. You wander in the air with your vision, while down on earth your wife and children or friends are deprived of their bread and their freedom.

I remember a man saying to me, "At last I did it. I left my family and children in the care of God, and now I am trying to find Him."

"You are a fool," I said. "If you ignore the God in your wife and children, you will never meet Him, except maybe in your hallucinations."

"But God said that we must leave our families and follow Him."

"He meant to leave your ego, yourself, and follow Him in the needs of others."

Vision is good, but it must be grounded in order to be effective.

7. When you develop your heart without your mind, you eventually become a careless person. People think that the heart makes you care for others. This is true. However, a parallel development of your heart and mind makes you a careful person, thus truly a caring person for others.

I remember going with a friend to the seashore and, as my friend pulled his boat into the ocean, I said, "The boat has a crack in the bottom. Water is coming in."

"Don't you have faith in God?" he asked.

"I have faith in God," I said, "but not in a cracked boat."

"That is very strange."

"Then you can go with your faith," I said to him.

He opened the sails and began to glide on the waves. Half an hour later he disappeared in the ocean with his "faith."

Self-deluded people think that they can do any stupid thing and blame God for it if they fail.

How Can You Start Developing Your Heart?

First, develop a sense of responsibility and then aspire toward beauty, purity, and joy.

The heart can be developed by rendering courageous and fearless service for humanity, by living an unselfish and heroic life, by deepening and expanding your love and making it more inclusive, and by feeling the pains of people and sharing their sufferings.

You can also develop the heart by visiting the sick and helping those who are failing in their lives.

You can develop your heart by coming in contact with the Christ and the Hierarchy.

Daily meditation is a very safe method to develop your heart, if it is done *with* the heart and *in* the heart.

Prayer, worship, and devotion to Great Ones make your heart bloom. Family relationships, group service, and even service to animals develop the heart.

One must start to develop the heart from childhood by cultivating respect, love, and gratitude. Gratitude is considered an adult quality, but children understand gratitude through their heart. Parents must not lose the opportunity to develop gratitude in the hearts of their children toward all of Nature and toward life as a whole. Gratitude opens the petals of the heart.

Once the heart is unfolded, reasoning and mental modifications cannot defeat it.

From childhood, people must be taught about the battle between the heart and the power of rationalization. They must be instructed how to protect the heart from the attacks of rationalization.

Developing the Heart and the Mind Together

The heart must be developed with the mind. Unless the mind is developed, the progress of a person will be incomplete.

The development of the mind is carried on especially through scientific thinking, the study of physics, chemistry, mathematics, history, and politics. Duties, responsibilities, and positions can develop the mind. Children must be given the opportunity to have certain positions in the family and to feel responsible for certain duties.

Both the heart and mind can be developed by dedicating oneself to creative arts such as painting, composing music, sculpting, etc. Sacred dances tremendously help the development of the heart and mind together.

It is interesting to note that science has created various methods to measure mental capacities, but up until now no apparatus has been created to measure the heart qualities. The heart is as real as the mind. A high I.Q. is not a sign that a person has a developed heart.

The heart and the mind are divided into two sections. The higher mind is the field of abstract thoughts, the receiver of Intuitional Light and impressions coming from Higher Worlds, while the lower mind is related to ordinary life, the mechanism of concrete knowledge and practical details of life. But if the whole mind is not aided by the developing heart, it becomes a sphere of crystallized dogmas, doctrines, and various thoughtforms.

The higher heart is the Chalice of the Flame of Life, the contact point of the Cosmic Magnet, and the source of all virtues. The lower heart is related to the solar plexus and to all negative emotions. Purification of the heart is a symbolic way to say that the lower heart is in the process of fusion with the higher heart. Once the lower heart is fused with the higher heart, it turns into a source of sympathy, fondness, and sensitivity.

The fusion of the heart with the mind creates a tremendous light which evokes the spirit, or the Core, of the human being. Pure will does not manifest until the person dedicates his mind and his heart to the upliftment of humanity. Before such an achievement, the will is an urge, a drive, a glamor, an illusion, a desire, but not pure will.

The fusion of the mind and heart eliminates from the human nature all those elements which are contradictory to the Cosmic Will. As man identifies himself with the Cosmic Will, he develops willpower. It is this willpower that directs his activities toward self-perfection.

When the heart and mind have a parallel development, the human soul enters the path of perfection and blooms day after day with light and beauty. The secret of such a blooming is that when the heart and mind develop together, they evoke the higher potentials of the mind and of the heart and the spiritual will which exists in the Core of every human being. This is how the *direction* is found.

The higher aspects of the heart cannot be developed without the striving of the mind. And the higher, creative aspects of the mind cannot be developed without the striving of the flame of the heart. When both the heart and mind are striving for greater and greater achievements, the greater light of the Divine Presence in man dawns in them. The mind, the heart, and the Presence work as a sacred trinity in the form of *beauty, goodness, and righteousness*, or in the form of *will, love, and light*. This is how a person achieves balance and equilibrium.

When the heart and the mind are developed simultaneously, the following factors come into existence:

1. You become idealistic but also practical. Idealism comes from the heart; practicality issues from the mind. When they are combined, you do not lose your soul in matter nor your path in Space.

Through idealism you create a great transformation in your nature; you create concentration toward supreme values. Through practicality you bring higher values into manifestation; you become a bridge between Higher Worlds and lower worlds, between the worlds of cause and effect.

2. When your heart and mind are developed simultaneously, you become intuitive and also intelligent. Intuition is a heart quality. Intelligence is a fiery mental quality. When both are united, you become guided by spiritual values, and you develop the ability to introduce these values to humanity in acceptable ways. Your light penetrates the darkness, thus helping people find their way toward the Source of Light.

3. When the heart and mind are cultivated simultaneously, you develop the power or the sense of synthesis and analysis. In synthesis, all parts are clear in the beauty of the whole. You think in terms of wholes, but you do not neglect any part which contributes to the whole. You can synthesize ideas, events, and information in all departments of human endeavor after passing all of them through the sphere of your analytical mind.

Analysis means to find the correct notes. Synthesis is the act of using these pure notes for a symphony. The heart synthesizes, the mind analyzes, and the *will* uses them for greater and greater achievements. Those who analyze but cannot synthesize always keep their noses in matter.

4. When the heart and mind are developed simultaneously, you become both highly sensitive and highly creative. The heart senses; the mind creates. Sensitivity makes you enjoy great beauties; creativity helps people share your joy.

Sensitivity is not an emotional quality only. It is also mental and spiritual. It is the power to record higher impressions which can be manifested in various ways through creativity.

5. When the heart and the mind are cultivated simultaneously, you develop feelings and the power to explain your feelings. Feelings come from the heart when the heart shares the aspirations, joys, strivings, pains, and sufferings of others. You can find the nature of the feeling and the source of the feeling and explain it through service, compassion, or an active participation with the same feeling.

Those who do not have feelings become dry, indifferent, and crude. Those who have feelings develop a sense of responsibility, sharing, and understanding. One can develop his power to explain the recorded feelings which are sometimes very subtle, fast, and complex. But a developed mind can follow the feelings and see the source. The heart feels; the intellect explains.

6. When the heart and mind are developed simultaneously, you become all-giving but also highly discriminative and righteous. You become righteous in relation to people, times, cycles, levels, conditions, etc. You do not give "guns" to criminals. Neither do you take away the "guns" of those who are protecting the freedom of humanity. You do not give twenty-five cents to an alcoholic begging for a handout, but you spend thousands to send a young man to college or to build a school or a hospital. You are ready to give your life if you can save thousands of lives.

7.   When the mind and the heart are developed simultaneously, you work for the freedom of mankind, but you see all existing limitations. You do not look at the stars and fall into the mud. You know that freedom is gained step by step, overcoming on each step a physical, emotional, or mental limitation. For you, freedom is not a concept or a feeling but a heavy responsibility. People can achieve freedom not by escaping from their duties and responsibilities but by facing them and fulfilling them.

Freedom is not something that we can give to others. Every one of us can achieve freedom in the degree of the expansion of our consciousness and transformation of our nature. Premature freedom destroys those who are not ready to meet the responsibilities presented by their freedom.

Neither the mind nor the heart can separately achieve freedom. Both the mind and the heart together must achieve freedom. As long as the heart is not pure or the mind is contaminated by past crimes, no freedom can be achieved. But those who develop their mind and heart simultaneously will achieve freedom and turn into paths to make others achieve freedom.

The balance between the heart and the mind leads to success. When the heart and mind are developed together, the will aspect of man emerges and becomes the power station behind the heart and the mind.

8.   Those who cultivate their heart and mind simultaneously develop a deep sense of beauty and

an intense urge for knowledge. Beauty and knowledge evoke the Divine Will in man and put It into action.

Beauty belongs to all, and knowledge is open to all those who will use it for the service of humanity. When man misuses his knowledge, the light of knowledge withdraws itself and darkness descends upon the planet.

It is the heart that searches for beauty; it is the mind that searches for knowledge; but it is the will that paves the way for the manifestation of beauty and knowledge as inseparable wings of the transformed human being.

Such a person does not betray the principle of beauty in any of his expressions, and he does not pass his knowledge to those who would use it for their separative interests.

Without the development of the heart, man attains knowledge, but he uses it for his own and for others' destruction.

There are people who accumulate knowledge of the Scriptures and the Teaching. They develop encyclopedic information in their mind, but they live a life of separatism, hatred, jealousy, malice, and slander. Then they justify their attitudes by the "wisdom" they have in their mind. The accumulated Wisdom of the Ages can be lived only when the heart has a high degree of development.

When the heart and mind are developed harmoniously, the person develops fearlessness, courage, and patience, and in the meantime a sense of timing and preciseness.

Such a person does not rush like a bull toward a red flag but takes his time, examines, decides the moment of action, and takes well-planned steps with courage and fearlessness. Patience is the fulcrum of the balance between the heart and mind.

When there is harmonious development between the heart and mind, victory is unavoidable. All failures are the result of the imbalance between the heart and mind. People fail because they use either their heart or their mind rather than both simultaneously.

9. Those who develop their heart and mind simultaneously clearly see the needs of humanity and take action. The needs are seen by the heart, and action is taken by the mind. If the action is taken for superficial reasons, it means that the mind is ahead of the heart, and the heart does not have the needed courage to produce the action.

All uplifting, transforming, and sublimating actions originate from the heart.

It is important to cultivate the heart of people if we want to see a world entering into beauty and inspiration. It is important also to cultivate their mind to actualize the dreams of the heart.

To let our heart unfold, we must watch over our thoughts. The heart can be poisoned by our ugly thoughts. The more lofty our thoughts, the greater the opportunity for our heart to unfold and bloom.

All thoughts that are harmful, separative, that are charged with fear, hatred, jealousy, treason, slander, and self-interest, must be dismissed, and we must not tolerate such ugly thoughts to take root within us and increase like weeds.

Every ugly thought hurts our heart and damages its energy network. Accumulated poison from ugly thoughts spreads into the heart, into the body, and makes the future existence of people devoid of happiness and joy.

Ugly thoughts also create disintegration of the aura. No one can keep his magnetism in the family and in groups once the termites of ugly thoughts penetrate into his heart.

For the Ancients, the heart was the Holiest Temple in which the Most High dwells. It is in the presence of the Most High that the heart unfolds and radiates the fragrance of the Most High. The healing, transforming, uplifting heart is the rarest treasure one can have...or one can discover in others.

Once the thoughts are under the control of the heart, the mind turns into a servant. Then thoughts can move mountains, using the energy of the heart.

Invoke your heart when you start your daily duties, when you are enjoying yourself with a sacred labor, when life threatens you, when you find yourself at the gates of Infinity.

The most shaking events and the most shaking revelations can be assimilated only by the unfolding heart.

Once I saw a picture of a heart with two wings. I realized that it is our heart that has wings, and it is our heart that carries us through Space when we leave our bodies. Heartless people are like birds with broken wings.

When both heart and mind have a high degree of development, they are endowed with the sense of direction, and they respond to the light within.

At present, the world has no balance. We have knowledge, industry, science, and technology which are far ahead of the heart. In the meantime, masses of people are totally deprived of the power of their discrimination and intellect and are the slaves of technology, science, and the rulers of the world. Most of these people are intoxicated with cults, religions, or a life of pleasures and slavery.

Masses of people, even in democratic countries, are slaves under the conditions created by the intellectuals. There are only a minority who have both the heart and mind developed. People cannot deceive such people, exploit them, or urge them to be slaves. The salvation of humanity lies in the hands of this minority, if their voices are heard. They are those who carry out the sacred duty of unifying mankind and leading it toward freedom, prosperity, and greater spiritual achievements.

A long time ago the human being was symbolized by a flaming heart. People think that the heart is a mechanism like the mind. The truth is that the heart is the abode of the Self. To develop the heart means gradually to be aware of the One Self, to bring your inner, real Essence into operation and expression.

Actually, as the heart and mind develop and reach a state of maturity, the heart absorbs the mind and acts as pure reason, pure love, and pure will, like a diamond with three facets.

❦   *Heart and Virtues*

Virtues are related to the heart. For many centuries man has forgotten about the heart and has emphasized the development of the mind for science, industry, and technology. Without the development of the heart, the mind prepares the most dangerous trap ever realized in the history of humanity.

Man is now trapped in the network of so-called inventions, industry, and science. The pollution of the air, water, and earth is so great that if we were to stop creating pollution at this time, it would still take us perhaps another seven hundred years to clean the planet.

The greatest trap, which is going to be the hardest to clear away, is the increasing belt of radioactivity and pollution around the planet. If this radioactivity and pollution come a few miles closer to the planet, we may face an immediate and grave disaster. This condition is what many of our colleges and universities and the technology of our age have produced. The heart was forgotten, and the people of the world did not use the light of their hearts to prevent the danger in which we find ourselves today.

The heart never lets the mind think in a way that will produce anti-survival factors in the world. The heart balances the thinking, brings equilibrium to it, and leads it toward those paths which guarantee the survival of life forms on this planet and in Space.

When the mind thinks, plans, or creates, the heart asks, "Is it good for everyone's survival?"

The mind says, "Who cares about everyone else? The important thing is me, my interests."

The heart says, "If something is not good for everyone, it is not good for you."

The mind answers, "Who cares about everyone else? Let me accumulate things and enjoy life."

The heart says, "One cannot enjoy life unless he shares the things he has. Only in sharing can one enjoy life."

Thus, the heart balances the mind.

When the mind makes new discoveries, the heart asks, "Is this invention going to hinder or help the future progress and well-being of humanity and the planet?"

And the minds answers, "Who cares about the future? Let us enjoy the present moment. Let us eat, drink, and have a good time and not worry about the future."

The heart then says, "If you do not care about the future, you do not have a future. Not to have a future means to die or to prepare a life of suffering and pain. Our civilization is killing the earth which humanity needs to have for the future."

The mind says, "Never mind about the future. Let us make money now."

The heart answers, "What about the children of tomorrow? How are they going to survive if we continue to pollute the waters, the earth, and the air? What about fifty years from now when grandchildren will come to their grandfathers and ask, 'What did you do for our planet? We don't have clean air to breathe, clean water to drink, or clean food to eat.' Grandfather will answer, 'But we lived a good life in the past, and now it is your turn to create something out of nothing.' "

The heart stands for survival and for life. Everything the heart expresses is for life, for everyone.

Knowledge and technology can be used for the destruction of humanity if the heart does not enlighten the mind. The enlightenment of the mind does not come from increased knowledge but from the increasing love of the heart.

The mind without the heart is separative, selfish, and earthbound, but the heart is inclusive, selfless, and space-bound.

When we speak of the heart, specifically, we refer to the etheric heart center. This center has one fire but twelve flames. Each flame radiates a particular kind of energy called a virtue. Actually, these flames are currents of energy which have the various names of virtues.

Each flame emanates from the Core of the human being. The heart center is like a lotus bud, and as we exercise a particular virtue, the corresponding petal of the bud slowly opens. This is the right way to activate and open the heart center.

An open heart center balances the person. All that he thinks, does, feels, and speaks is for the good of all humanity, for the good of all living beings. When the heart does not work, the mind becomes selfish, separative, and criminal. When the heart begins to operate, the selfishness of the mind disappears and the mind works in terms of inclusiveness. Separativeness becomes unity. Crime turns into an urge to serve all humanity.

What Do the Virtues Do?

1. Each virtue coming from the Core of the human soul brings life-electricity to the mental, emotional, and physical natures of man. This electricity energizes and heals the threefold nature of man.

A person of virtue makes the right decision at the right moment. A person of vice cannot make the right decision at the right time, and he fails in his life. The decision to be virtuous is pro-survival. The decision to be a person of vice is anti-survival.

A virtuous person is more successful, progressive, and creative than a person of vices. Vices block the energies coming from your Core and make you the slave of the forces coming from the environment. Vices block your vision, your thinking, your sense of timing, and the flow of your energy resources. But when you increase in virtues, they make you fearless and courageous. They make you strive.

2. Any virtue establishes a connection between your physical, emotional, and mental natures and your future. Every virtue stands for the future. Vices are for the past. Virtues lead you to future achievements.

Vices are forces used for your immediate pleasures. Your future is what you want to be as a spiritual beauty. Your future is your unfolded state of beingness. Your future is the culmination of all the dreams and visions of your soul.

Virtues bring in energy. They build your foundation, they build your future, and they create striving to make you transcend yourself.

Vices weaken you, exhaust your energy, and deform you. Any vice brings distortion within your organs and glands and changes your manners, voice, and look. Virtues make you shine and radiate beauty.

3. Virtues decrease your karmic taxations. For example, you did many wrong things — mentally, emotionally, and physically — and they accumulated, becoming a karmic burden on your shoulders. When you practice virtues, you accumulate so much wealth that you pay your karmic debts automatically without suffering and pain.

Let us say that your karma is equal to a five thousand dollar fine; if you do not pay, you will suffer the consequences. But before the punishment arrives, if you make five hundred thousand dollars with your virtues, you are able to pay the five thousand dollars without feeling any tension.

This is why we must also think about good, speak about good, and act for the good. Good increases our wealth, and in the darkest hours of our lives it pays our debts.

From childhood I had a tendency or urge to help people. I remember once spending half a day to bring medicine to an elderly woman. Another time, I spent one whole day bringing down a cat which had climbed to the highest branch of a big tree and was very frightened. I used to help neighbors in any way I could. In school I used to help children not only from my class, but also from lower and higher classes.

Once my mother said to me, "You are always doing good for others." I think that doing good saved me from many karmic debts and serious dangers which I passed through without the slightest scratch. I remember once being carried away by the tides of a river, and someone jumped in and saved me. A great bear once came out of the forest and slept next to me without hurting me. One time I was accidentally locked in the furnace of a locomotive engine, and someone happened to open the door through curiosity and found me there. I walked away from many car accidents without being hurt. I assume that doing good for others is the best way to pay our karmic debts and increase our savings.

There was a man who used to help people in any way possible. He made lots of friends. Years passed, and he lost all his possessions in an earthquake. He traveled to various cities to find a job. In every city he found people who invited him to stay at their home for a few days. He was never left without shelter and food. Finally, an old man whom he had helped ten years earlier, gave him all his real estate, his home, and all that he had. The man eventually realized that no one can lose anything if it is the result of his sweat and labor, and if he has a karmic savings account.

A virtue is a source of blessing.

4. Virtues increase your magnetism. You attract creative forces in Nature to cooperate with you in your labor. You attract the right people, the right friends, and the right events and conditions in your life. People who lose their magnetism by living in vices eventually find themselves abandoned by people and by the creative forces in Nature.

Each virtue adds to your magnetism. We have twelve virtues of the heart. Christ chose twelve disciples, symbolizing the twelve virtues of the heart. It is these twelve virtues that, through their magnetism, have brought great changes on earth.

Each disciple also represented a zodiacal constellation. He represented the energy of his constellation and transmitted that energy through a virtue. Christ was the Central Core of the Zodiac of the disciples who, like a mighty magnet, were transmitting, transmuting, transforming, and transfiguring energies from Cosmic Sources.

Each one of us can change into a magnet and increase goodness on earth through developing virtues. People will come to you and help you actualize your vision and reach your dreams if you develop virtues.

5. Virtues heal your body. In the future, physicians are going to prescribe a virtue for you before they give you medicine. In the future, it will be clearly known that most sicknesses are the result of vices or the absence of virtues. They will discover which virtue is related to the heart, the liver, etc., and prescribe it for you. If you want to have a healthy life, you will develop virtues.

Virtues give you resistance and immunity to microbes and germs. Vices create in your body those conditions which help germs and microbes or viruses multiply.

Some years ago a beautiful, healthy, and happy man came to see me for some business. A few months later I saw him again. He was unhealthy, unhappy, and very depressed.

"What happened to you," I asked.

"Well, I fell into the habit of using drugs, and I lost all that I had."

Vices lead us to physical and moral destruction, while virtues bring us energies from Higher Sources which in turn give us vitality, joy, and sanity. Virtues even give us strength in times of crisis. A virtuous person keeps his mental, emotional, and physical health in times of serious crises, while others lose their mind.

Vices are anti-survival factors. For example, if a thirteen-year-old girl runs after her sexual satisfaction and dopes herself, it is easy to see what her future will be.

The sunny days of the future are the result of our virtuous lives.

6. Virtues make you ready to be used by the Great Ones, the Hierarchy, first unconsciously, then consciously. It is the greatest success in life if you are used by Great Ones to promote the Plan to establish the foundation of a better life on earth.

One may ask, "Am I ready to be a co-worker of all constructive forces in Nature? Am I ready to be a staff member in the office of a Great One? What are my qualifications and what is my merit?" Virtues make you ready, in many different ways, to be called for a higher duty and responsibility.

There was a monastery in Asia which accepted students only after examining them physically, emotionally, and mentally. Physically they had to be good looking and healthy. They used to make you run 10-15 miles, swim for a few hours, and climb a mountain at a fast pace to discover if your body was healthy.

Emotionally they expected you to be fearless, joyful, and full of aspiration. To find out about all this, they used to create conditions in which your true colors would come out.

Mentally they expected you to have the love of beauty and a mind with a searching and penetrating quality, a mind that could visualize and create.

They used to hate gossipy and touchy boys, or those who were full of self-pity. The Teachers used to say that when they accepted a student, they considered him to be the flower of past virtues and the promise of future beauty.

Virtues make us ready to be used for labor in the field of life.

I remember a very old Teacher taking me to the mountains for a walk. After a few hours we were passing a dangerous curve in the mountain. He began to talk very enthusiastically, catching my whole attention, until he realized that I had noticed a man lying on the hillside.

"Teacher," I said, "there is a man there. Maybe he needs help."

"Well, you are not listening to my words, and you are interested in a fool who has fallen there."

"But...."

I jumped down the hill, and seeing that the man was almost dying, I managed to pull him up to the road and carry him on my back for almost half a mile to a fountain where I thought he could find rest.

When we were close to the fountain, he jumped off my back and began to dance. With great surprise I looked at my Teacher who was silently following me.

"Well," he said, "you passed the test of compassion."

We all have encountered hundreds of such tests in our lives to prove our many virtues, and whoever passes the tests makes himself ready for a greater responsibility. Great Ones are waiting for those who make themselves ready for such sacrificial service.

7. Virtues make you ready to come in contact with subjective centers of wisdom, joy, and vision. These centers are called Ashrams. They are found

on the Intuitional Plane, where a person can penetrate if virtues crown his head.

Virtues raise your vibration, expand and transmute your consciousness, and bring currents of creative inspiration into your soul. As virtues unfold, the pure life hidden in your Core radiates out, purifies your whole nature, and makes you ready to tune in to great Centers of wisdom in the Universe.

A virtuous person is continuously in contact with the creative ideas and plans of Ashrams. It is through such contact that he becomes a leader and a servant of light.

8. Virtues literally transmute the substance of your bodies. As the virtues bring more and higher energy into your system, they make the cells and atoms of your bodies advance and radiate more light and energy. Eventually all your bodies are built with the finest elements to such a degree that, together, they form a field of pure fire in which no unclean physical, emotional, or mental element can penetrate.

Transfiguration is the highest state gained through developing the virtues. Your bodies turn into light as the Inner Sun radiates through the virtues. Transfigured bodies can survive the greatest tensions and gain strength because of the tensions.

The fire that is released at the time of Transfiguration is called the fire of spirit, creative fire, or psychic energy. The Christians call it the Holy Spirit, which was in existence before this world came into being. This fire of spirit not only integrates and transfigures the personality, but it also opens the channel of communication with Higher Worlds and higher sources of beauty and wisdom.

Virtues expand the consciousness, and as the consciousness expands, the vehicles try to adapt themselves to the expanding consciousness. If the bodies do not live the virtues, they crack and face many kinds of troubles. It is in the process of adaptation of the bodies to the expanding consciousness that sublimation in the bodies takes place.

9. Virtues energize our etheric, astral, and mental centers and senses. The senses develop in proportion to our increasing virtues. If we live the twelve virtues of the heart, our senses will stay perfect to the end and will then lead us to conscious immortality because senses are bridges between various worlds.

Most of our senses are blocked because of our vices. When we replace vices with virtues, we will see a great improvement in the functioning of our senses.

Senses are also our creative agents. They receive the finest impressions if they are highly developed. And when highly developed, they can translate these impressions into our lives in the best way possible. Without the development of our senses, we cannot be creative. Senses receive the seeds of light and cause them to bloom as creative expressions. Virtues not only make the senses extremely sensitive to higher impressions, but they also protect the senses from attacks of crime, ugliness, and darkness. Undeveloped senses have no power to reject ugliness, but a developed sense of hearing, for example, can immediately reject a flat note.

10. Virtues make you beautiful, not only physically but also emotionally and mentally. As the Inner Core unfolds through virtues, it harmonizes all your bodies and gradually brings them closer to the likeness of your Divine Archetype. You can see tremendous beauty emanating from the thoughts, emotions, and deeds of the great Teachers of humanity.

Beauty, like a magnet, attracts people. People feel the inner beauty in others, and they try to make themselves beautiful in order to be able to relate to the beauty they see or feel. A virtuous person spreads beauty through his thoughts, words, and manners.

Virtues are like streams of pure water which turn a field into a meadow of flowers.

11. Virtues make you a source of blessing. If you have virtues, you strengthen, purify, and give pure joy.

12. Virtues make your transition a happy and blissful event. You attract pure and beautiful entities around you. Your Solar Angel guides and protects you. You feel detached from all worldly ties. You feel secure and protected in the next worlds. Your senses immediately operate in the subtle planes. You enjoy the immortality of life.

Even if you pass through painful experiences before death, you feel happy knowing that you are getting rid of the dark karma you created in the past, or that you are paying the karmic taxes of your many beloved ones.

We are told that those people who are full of vices enter the subtle planes as if they were blind.

❦　　*Radiation of the Heart*

People think that only our eyes are affected by light. In reality, even our skin and hair cells are very sensitive to light, color, and sound. But the most sensitive organ to light, color, and sound is our heart. Every change in the elements of light, color, and sound produces corresponding reactions and responses in the heart.

Our heart is the central organ in our relationships, and as the heart changes, our relationships change. Every human being with whom we have contact is known to our heart as a color image. Any disturbances felt in the color image of the person create repulsion in our heart. For example, if a person is a hypocrite, or has a bad motive behind his smiles, our heart registers this as a conflicting sensation and repels the person. But often we do not follow the indications of our heart.

Second, if a person lives in an environment that has colors which conflict with his color image, people do not feel friendly toward him because they feel a conflict in his presence. But if that same person is present in another environment that has colors which harmonize with his color image, people will like him.

When you have a friend who is in an environment that fits his color image, your heart is attracted to him. But if he is in an environment where his color image does not fit, you feel negative toward him. This negativity calls forth from your sub-conscious mind memories of accidents, ill feelings, failures, defeats, etc. Color, light, and sound affect the heart.

Everyone is impressed by two color images. One color image is an overall radiation, or the color that emanates from our Core, our beingness. Our key color is the color of our beingness.

The second color image comes into being when two people meet for the first time in a place which has a distinctive color.

For example, I see someone dressed in red standing in a yellow painted room. His color image which impresses itself on my mind is yellow-red, and my image of him is yellow-red plus the color of my dress.

Our heart registers both images simultaneously. The color image of a person's beingness, or of the radiation of his Core, is an invisible color, but it exists and impresses our heart. The second color image is visible, but even though we are often unconscious of it, it still impresses our heart.

As we have harmonics in music, we have also the harmonics of color. This means certain colors of other people do not harmonize with our colors or with the color of the particular environment.

If you meet anyone in a yellow colored environment who is dressed in yellow, and if your color image of beingness does not tune in with the color of the environment, you and he will feel rejection or a discord. But if the colors agree, both of you feel an inner rapport, love, or attraction.

You can develop your sensitivity consciously and dress in the proper colors for special occasions. For example, if you are visiting someone for business, you must know what color the environment has and dress in harmony with that color. Success is inevitable if your color image harmonizes with the environment.

Also, if the color of your beingness does not tune in to the color of your house, office, or clothes, you weaken your vitality.

If you observe and research, you can find the colors that are helpful on various occasions. The best way to find the right color for you is to develop the sensitivity of your heart which instantaneously tells you what color to wear when and what colors must be in your home or office.

The color image of your beingness changes when the focus of your consciousness shifts from level to level. If this happens, the former color does not necessarily remain helpful to you.

Colors have their life span; some are long-lived, some are short-lived. At certain times, we link certain color images to certain colors. For example, if we are talking about a person while always in a room that has antagonistic colors to his color image, very soon that color image will fade away. But if we are talking or thinking about that person in an environment which is harmonious with his color image, that color image will live much longer in our memory.

People have their key color images, and their health and happiness are controlled by those colors that reach them from the sun through the atmosphere. Pollution prevents certain colors from sufficiently reaching us, and sometimes we receive an overdose of some colors because of accumulating or dispersing layers of pollution in the atmosphere and ozone holes.

If we knew the science of colors, we would travel to those places where we could have more sympathetic colors from the sun or from the environment.

If we study our heart, we will see that there are slight or major changes in our heart in various places on earth. We can have our heart guide us in choosing places to live.

Cells are very sensitive to light, color, and sound. Man also is a cell on the planet, and he too is affected. In the future, people will use color to heal humanity of its psychic sicknesses...or to kill humanity with color rays.

Many books are written about colors and many people are working with them, but the science is still in its infancy.

Light, color, and sound affect the heart. If we measure the heartbeat and observe the changes of the beat under the effect of different sounds and colors and light, we will have some precious discoveries to use for healing the disorders of the heart and, through the heart, other disorders of the body.

In the near future the colors of schools, public places, and houses will be designed scientifically to improve the health of people. The main consideration will be *color, form,* and *sound.* Form will be recognized as substantiation and objectification of sound, and color will be recognized as the radiation of sound. These colors, sounds, and forms will be chosen in accordance with the type and quality of the heart of the residents. The correct lighting will also be chosen.

Every heart is the same in essence, but each may have different rays in different stages of evolution. Every heart is the manifestation of the human soul. This is why the heart, if pure, knows how to choose color, sound, and form.

Advanced souls choose to work in natural light, or the light of a wax candle or wood — preferably pine, eucalyptus, and oak. We are told that Masters use Their own light, the light of Their soul. Thus darkness has no control over Them.

There are two major ways to use color, sound, and form properly and continually. One is a scientific method using various electronic devices. The other method is to use the heart. A pure heart is the most dependable instrument.

The heart can choose the right color, the right light, the right sound, and the right form and make a person healthy, happy, enlightened, and victorious — if that person obeys his heart.

In the future, one of the major fields of study will be the study of heart. Medical science is now very advanced in knowledge about the nature of the physical heart. But it is not knowledgeable about the invisible petals of the heart, the invisible flame of the heart, and their relationship to our health, actions, emotions, thoughts, visions, and future.

A developing heart will be the best communication device between man and man, between the planet and man, between the Solar System and man.

The heart will be able not only to reflect the conditions of the human body but also the actions of humanity, the planet, and the Solar System. The heart will also be sensitive to great opportunities created in the Cosmos and utilize them for the benefit of all.

A developing heart in itself will be the source of the light that man needs, the source of color and sound by which he will cause changes in his environment. The heart will produce enough heat to warm the form of man when he is cold, and it will cool man when he is hot.

The heart will also provide vital food for man by absorbing light, color, and sound that can be transformed into energy in his system.

The heart is the best communications device ever created. Once it is unfolded, it will be able to communicate with planetary, solar, and even with galactic environments. It is the most complex recording instrument ever known in the world.

It is obvious that this instrument, the heart, is a gift given to man from the Higher Worlds. It serves as an information center for the Higher Worlds. The

Higher Worlds *read* our heart to know all that is necessary to know about our life.

This gift is given to us to use. We can use it to unfold deeper potentials hidden within us, or we can destroy it and fail in our purpose in life.

The stories about perfect human beings, called Masters, are not legends but facts. Every human being is a master if he compares himself with other life-forms. Why would human development stop if such a dynamo is placed in man's nature?

It is fascinating to think that the human Core used the light of the Sun, the Zodiac, and the stars to build his physical, emotional, and mental mechanisms. He used color and also fragrance, but most of his achievements were based on the strivings of his heart.

It was the light of the Sun that activated the Spark. It was the light of the Solar Angel that activated his intelligence. It was the Heart of the Sun that provided compassion, and through these lights, the human Core made himself more independent, age after age.

The time will come when he will be the light for lesser kingdoms, or for newly developing human souls. He will be the source building their heart and activating their intellect until they also step on the path of perfection. The heart within man is the vanguard for all their progress and for future progress beyond our present understanding.

The heart, the Hierarchy, and intense individual aspiration are three factors which will create the future *giants* of humanity. They will be spiritual giants, fully equipped to live in harmony with cosmic currents of life — one with the Cosmic Heart.

In the heart there is the sound, there is the light, and there are the twelve currents of colors.

Each feeling of the heart is a release of a current of color. That is why the heart is so inclusive. It talks, it enlightens, it heals and regenerates. Great Hearts are streams of twelve colors which make a person appear as a rainbow with twelve colors.

The communication of the heart is through the "Voice of Silence." Every heart can hear such a voice in different sensations. This voice puts the heart in direct and pure communication — if the heart is not polluted with self-interest and separatism.

Every heart emanates twelve streams of light — with their specific colors.

The heart not only communicates with human hearts, but if it is trained and advanced in its unfoldment, it also communicates with the heart of every living form, the heart of the planet, and the Heart of the Sun.

The twelve petals of the heart are twelve flames, twelve lights, twelve colors, and twelve sounds which, as a totality, receive energies from Space and transmit them into the environment. Great is the power of the heart.

Exercises to Develop the Heart

- Try every day, for the whole of your life, to infuse your thoughts, emotions, words, and actions with compassion, joy, and freedom.

- Stand on the foundation of harmlessness and strive toward the future.

- Visualize your heart as a Chalice from the center of which radiate twelve streams of energy, with twelve separate colors. See yourself as blue, yellow, or ruby. Visualize your center or Chalice in front of your eyes, four inches away from your forehead.

This visualization can be done

— two minutes daily for only a month

— three minutes daily for six months

— four minutes daily for another five months

— ten minutes daily for the remaining years of your physical life

During this exercise "visualize" hearing the word *AUM* as coming from the Core of your heart.

- Once you feel that the sensitivity of your heart is increasing, try to keep your body healthy, your emotions pure, and your mind occupied with lofty ideas and creative actions.

This exercise can bring abundant blessings in your life.

❧   *Heart and Impressions*

A time comes in our life when higher senses begin to function properly, and they transmit their recordings to our heart, bypassing our physical senses.[1]

The heart has various levels in its power of registration. All subtle senses are related to the heart. We hear, touch, see, smell, or taste in subtle planes, but our physical senses do not record them. Only our heart, if it is pure, registers impressions from higher realms and translates them into subtle feelings which have no vocabulary yet. As a package, we often call them joy, or anguish, but such

---

1. Higher senses are the astral and mental and even higher senses, the equivalents of the physical senses on higher planes. For further information on higher senses, please refer to *Challenge for Discipleship, The Psyche and Psychism,* and *Other Worlds.*

words are sum totals of various feelings not discerned by the sense organs of the physical body.

It is sometimes necessary to analyze our joys and anguishes to see how many threads of feelings are woven into them. The consciousness of a person is not always developed enough to discriminate between these threads, but the heart sees them as they are; and the consciousness can ponder upon their effects if it is purified enough.

Some people express such sensations through their tears. In every tear drop we can find the expression of these threads of feelings. As multifaceted crystals, tears transmit the various colors of these threads while our physical senses are often deeply busy with their physical interests.

It is important for "travelers" to have moments in which they record the subtle messages of threads. They may offer new avenues in the understanding of human nature and the Higher Worlds and provide new fields of discovery in the relationship between man and Cosmos.

Most of the joy reaching our shores is registered in our heart. Anguish is registered in our solar plexus. Often these two centers are in conflict with each other, creating more complicated sets of sensations.

Some currents received contain universal messages. Each of these messages touches our highest aspirations, visions, and future and part of them comes to us through the solar plexus. They become translated in distorted ways and make the personality feel the anguish, but the soul rejoices. It is seldom that the personalty understands the joy of the soul. And it is seldom that the heart and solar plexus resound in unison.

Here again man can feel a cleavage within himself. The mountains in his nature can be bathed in the light of the sun, but the valleys of his nature remain in deep darkness. This must be a temporary state. The impressions coming from Higher Worlds and the impressions coming from physical realms must cooperate with each other.

The higher impressions must eventually be recorded by our lower senses. This will enable us to bring the guidance and wisdom from the Higher Worlds. The senses on the lower planes must go through a process of refinement. Such a refinement is possible through expanding our consciousness and purifying our heart. The impressions coming from the lower realms must eventually be recorded by higher senses.

We do not always have fully unfolded higher senses. Often they are in a *seed* stage or in a damaged condition. Wrong and harmful emotions damage astral senses and make them incapable of registering higher impressions. Wrong and harmful thoughts damage mental senses and make them incapable of receiving higher impressions.

Damaged senses produce friction within themselves and send broken currents of force to their corresponding centers, producing false alarms, false messages coming from either lower or Higher Worlds. Man is always mislead in his life when he is in such a condition.

Intuitional and atmic centers are in full bloom because they belong to the Solar Angel. It is our relationship with our Solar Angel that helps us receive higher impressions and register them with our physical, emotional, and mental senses in proportion to their unfoldment.

Before the Solar Angel leaves us in the Fourth Initiation, we must have our higher senses built in order to inherit the vehicles of the Solar Angel as a "reward" for letting It eventually be free.

It is interesting to note that our heart has a direct link with the higher senses and with the Higher Worlds. That is why our heart registers impressions that bypass our senses. The heart registers not only impressions from our astral and mental realms but also from the Higher Worlds.

Endeavoring to listen, observe, and analyze the recordings or feelings of the heart leads us to the path of refinement.

The cleavage between our higher senses and lower ones sometimes is bridged by certain devas — if we gain their friendship through the purity of our life, through the beauty of our thoughts, emotions, and actions.

Some very average persons, without a great unfoldment of their senses, have received higher impressions because of the purity, beauty, and simplicity of their lives. In such cases, devas bridged the gap existing in their nature. But this does not last if the person fails to unfold his mind or becomes loaded with the problems of the world.

Great Ones suggest that the Highest Guide within comes through the heart. It is in the temple of the heart that the highest and the lowest meet.

Meditation and service build paths leading to the heart.

Harmlessness on the threefold levels of the personality purifies the heart. One can realize how much harm is done to one's own heart through past harmful thoughts, feelings, and actions. The heart has been wounded at various times, and it needs a long time to recover before it can reflect to us the splendor of the Higher Worlds.

C•H•A •P•T•E•R   8

❦   *Listening to the Heart*

    All ancient Sages have spoken about the heart.
They have said that the heart must control our
thoughts, our words, and our actions. The heart is
our conscience, our innermost consciousness.
    Before you think, or before you put your
thoughts into action, it is better to check with your
heart. Before you speak, check with your heart.
Before you take any action, it is best first to ask your
heart. You will see that your heart always leads you
into directions that will bring you health, happiness,
prosperity, enlightenment, and beauty. The mind
must be under the control of the heart to have right
direction. A great Sage says, "Each heart has direct
access to the Cosmic Heart." If you listen very carefully to your heart, you will never make mistakes.
    To listen to your heart does not mean to listen
to your emotions, your glamors, your desires, your

anger, etc. Sometimes we are confused about this. You must be silent and ask your heart if what you are thinking, speaking, and doing is really in harmony with the Cosmic Heart.

Of course, we cannot see the Cosmic Heart. The Cosmic Heart is the principle that created everything and is in everything. The Cosmic Heart impresses us with the *only* direction that we must find in order to be right, to be healthy, prosperous, enlightened, and beautiful. In every heart there is the presence of the Cosmic Heart.

Every time we escape from the whisper of our heart, we can see that we are trapped. The majority of the coming generation will be mostly followers of the heart. Their heart will not tolerate "monkey business," selfishness, and things that people do for their own physical, emotional, and mental interests — such as forgetting their promises, their love, and their duties. If people make contact with their heart, they will have the best friendships, the best groups, and the best nation. Their unity will be invulnerable because the heart gives strength. The heart gives guidance, and the heart gives light to do things in the right way and with right relationships.

Do not depend on your mind and intellect so much. When we observe world history, we see that those who wanted to destroy humanity used their mind and intellect, but not their heart. They poisoned our oceans, air, lakes, rivers, soil, trees, animals, and they poisoned us. They have done this by using their intellect, their mental powers to accumulate money, power, and control. But they have never gone to the door of their heart and asked, "Is what we are doing right?" If they had asked their heart, it would have answered, "Don't pollute this earth. Don't create wars, ammunitions, and germ warfare."

What kind of heartless leadership do we have throughout the world? If we want to go back and clean our atmosphere and relationships with people, there is only one place to go — to our heart. The heart is the *real* Eden. Your good health depends on your heart.

The Ancients had an interesting symbol. When they wanted to draw up a contract or give a promise, they would put their hand on their heart. This was the most sacred sign among primitive peoples because they had direct contact with the Universe. Their minds were not polluting them. It was also the sign that Initiates gave to each other. For example, the Hierarch would speak to the Initiate, or the Chief Knight would say to the knights, "Put your hand on your heart." Now say, "From now on I am going to serve humanity." They promised on their heart — the most sacred aspect of a person.

What is the heart we are referring to? We are speaking about the heart center. We are not talking about the physical heart. We are talking about the heart chakra that cannot be transplanted. Once you ruin it with selfishness, revenge, and hatred, you have ruined it forever.

The heart center has twelve petals. As you strive toward perfection and listen to your heart, the petals open, eventually forming a beautiful chalice. Each petal is an energy source which radiates a virtue. There are twelve virtues in your heart.

Virtue means power and energy, beauty, abundance, prosperity, radioactivity, and glory. A great Sage once said that in the history of all Great Ones, if you follow Their life path, you will never find an act that was against the heart. Regardless of what happened to Them, They stayed in the heart. Because They stayed in the heart, and all of their thoughts, words, and actions were emanations from the heart, They became Great Ones. The path to be a Great One is made by your efforts to communicate with your heart. The heart will eventually cause you to bloom and flourish.

In the twelve-petaled lotus at the center of the heart, we are told that there is a blue electric flame. As the petals open, the blue electric fire increases and increases. Eventually you have the source of magnetism, electricity, and power within you which, when combined, is called psychic energy. Psychic energy is the radiation of the flame of the heart. You have this within you, but it is sleeping until you develop it through your sacrificial, heartfelt actions, thoughts, and speech.

This central flame has three tongues. Each is a different color. The first tongue is called **enthusiasm**. The second is **self-sacrifice**, and the third is **striving**. As you unfold the twelve petals — the twelve virtues of the heart — the three tongues of the one flame start opening.

What does **enthusiasm** do for you? Enthusiasm connects you with the Cosmic Magnet. You start expanding your communication lines into Cosmos and find a direction that is the principle of life in the Universe. When you make that contact, your life is not dead, not shallow, not depressed; it is radiation. You do things with joy and great happiness. It is so contagious to have that fire. One person can mobilize a nation, if he or she has the fire of enthusiasm. We can see in the history of humanity a few people here and there who moved armies and nations with the flame of their heart.

What does **self-sacrifice** do? When we say self-sacrifice, people sometimes think, "I must put my neck here and let someone cut it off." We are not referring to this. *Real* self-sacrifice means to get rid of everything in your nature that is not God. Get rid of it! Get rid of every kind of trash in your life. When you do this, the greatest sacrifice, which is your Essence, appears. Man, in his Core, is sacrifice.

What are we doing here on this planet? You say that you are sacrificing in your suffering, pain, agony, war, blood, diseases and hospitals, injections and X rays. You love, she hates; she loves, you hate — separations, divorces, cheating each other. What is this? It is pain and suffering. But a sacrificial person slowly gives everything, and in giving everything he owns *himself*. Christ said to a disciple, "What will it profit you if you have the whole world in your pocket, but lose your soul?" This means that your soul, your Self, is the highest treasure you can have, but how can you find that soul? You find it by stripping the soul of all hypocrisy and of all that is not divine within you. Eventually the Jewel will be revealed. How beautiful it is when you relate to people with a clear conscience and with clear love, honesty, and beauty. The result will be tremendous happiness, joy, and bliss in your life.

Enthusiasm puts you in contact with the Cosmic Magnet. Self-sacrifice opens the gate for you to contact the Hierarchy. No one can enter into the Hierarchy or make a contact with Them without proving that his life is self-sacrificial. Unfortunately, in our universities, colleges, and various other institutions, we learn how to manipulate and cheat people. We have millions of self-interest diskettes. Whichever button you push, it starts self-interest. Sometimes you cannot even talk with people without giving them at least a small chance to have self-interest. Otherwise they will not listen to you. It is so important to contact those Great Ones and eventually feel that you are *somebody*.

I remember one day in the monastery being told that a highly respected Teacher was coming for a visit. Those who wanted to see him could do so. Automatically, the first thing I did was to change my clothes, shave, and start practicing a nice walk. I said, "I don't know how I am going to greet him." I went to my Teacher and asked, "How should I greet this Teacher?" He replied, "That is your business." "Don't leave me like this," I said. I walked for two or three minutes to see how I was walking. Then I asked, "If he looks at me, how will I feel?" My whole body was electrified. Then I said, "Let me go." I opened the door and looked at him. He looked at me. I walked toward him with confidence and took his hand and kissed it, then stood looking in his face. "Sit there," he said, as he put his hand on me. I said to myself, "Thank God no accident happened." I sat there while many others came and went. If that was facing a great Teacher, how are you going to face a great Master, a Great One? You can do it with only one thing — with proof that you sacrificed everything you could throughout the ages. Eventually you will get the "visa."

Striving is the determination to annihilate the limitations in which you are living. There are emotional limitations, hang-ups, the "I can't detach" limitation, the "I am stuck" limitation, the ignorance limitation, mental limitations, and limitations of your consciousness. There are limitations of hatred, jealousy, fear, anger, slander, malice, and treason. All of them are vipers eating you.

Striving is like a jet ascending through a deep layer of clouds, then finally emerging into the sunshine. Striving is to make your light stand above the clouds of your personality interests and chaos and be in the sunshine. Striving leads to the Tower, the Cosmic control center, so to speak. Once we have a contact with this Center, we are totally transformed human beings.

I recently read something very interesting. Helena Roerich wrote in her diary, "Tonight, with a Great One, I visited Shamballa." She was a young woman when she accompanied her husband high into the Himalayas for a long-lasting expedition. One day when their tents were set up in the valley she said, "I want to climb to that mountain peak." Later, M.M. wrote about that event with these words, "That was the symbolic spirit of Helena Roerich. She always strove to the heights." He called her "the Bird of the Heights." That striving slowly connects you with *the Center where the Will of God is known.*

Each of the three tongues of the flame of the heart is composed of many elements. The first, **enthusiasm,** is composed of *courage, daring, one-pointedness, patience, perseverance,* and *fiery action.* All of these things, in a package, compose enthusiasm. Wherever you see enthusiasm, there you will find courage and a dare-devil spirit, perseverance and patience. If you meditate on these points, you will find it very rewarding in your life. Richness of life can only be produced by meditating on these great principles.

Self-sacrifice, the second point of the flame, is formed of the following elements:

Compassion. Compassion is unlimited love, understanding, and calmness in any situation. You understand why a person is doing certain things. You understand why he is doing this, and you are not upset because you know the causes that are coming from five hundred years in the past. These causes are going to manifest, so why be upset? Compassion is not feeling. It is a real stage of consciousness in which you understand. You do not condemn people for acting in certain ways; you understand, and you love them.

Forgiveness. It is so beautiful to learn to forgive. Humanity is destroying itself because people do not have the power of forgiveness. Forgiveness is the understanding of causes and results simultaneously. Forgiveness is the feeling that the cause and the result must manifest to clear the way for the persons involved.

Gratitude. A self-sacrificing person is always grateful. As you sacrifice things that you are not, you come in contact with your innermost Self. This gives you a tremendous amount of gratitude. I have noticed that when that spirit, the feeling of gratitude, vanishes in a person, he or she always becomes selfish and self-destructive. Be grateful to your friends, to your wife or husband, to your teacher. Gratitude means to sacrifice things that are obscuring and hindering your contact with others.

Inclusiveness. Self-sacrifice is always inclusive. As we go toward our True Self, we become more inclusive. As we go down to the not-Self, we become selfish and separative. If men and women think only for themselves, there is no hope. They will always be unsuccessful because they are not inclusive.

Harmlessness. A self-sacrificing person is always harmless. He sacrifices himself instead of sacrificing others. We can see this in youth. Sometimes they manifest such a masterpiece quality. For example, a girl loved a boy, and she saw that another girl also loved that boy. Even though it was very painful for them to separate, she gave him up. She said, "I will gladly give up my relationship if you want the other girl." You are going to be harmless.

Intuition. The second point of the flame, self-sacrifice, is very intuitive. Before a person speaks, you know intuitively what is going on in his or her heart. You know how things are going to occur. You know if a plan, a conversation, or a contact will be creative or destructive. You feel it. If your heart is open, the first contact with a person tells you what is going to happen. But if your heart is not open, you are trapped. The most important thing in your life is to develop your heart to such a degree that you have a compass in the dark sea of life. Develop your heart with heartfelt actions.

Striving, the third point of the flame, is composed of five important elements: *daring, patience, persistence, endurance, and nobility.* All of these demands lead you to your Divinity and bring you good fortune. Today's ethic says, "If we do not cheat, we cannot make money." There was a man who opened a liquor store in a small town. I met with him and asked, "Why are you bringing this liquor here?" He replied, "Well, I want to create a business." For one year he had a good business. The next year he was seeing that everyone was going crazy and destroying his shop. One day several people drank and drank, then burned the shop and killed him. His brother told me, "You were right when you told him that kind of business wouldn't pay." Do things that will bring good fortune to others and to yourself.

Have persistence. The heart always persists. I know a woman whose husband was drinking day and night. She came to me and said, "I am going to persist in praying and praying for this man until only my bones remain." Eventually, her husband became such an angel. She was so proud that she had endured and persisted. Her vision and her dreams for her husband came true.

A great Sage has said the following regarding the heart:

> *The bond with the Higher Spheres is formed through your heart.*

If you do not have heart, you have no contact with Higher Spheres. If you do not have contact with Higher Spheres, you are lost in your life.

> *Those who wish to participate in Our Abode, must communicate with their heart.*

If you want to have greater guidance in your heart, in your mind, and in your feelings, slowly try to enter into the sphere of the electromagnetic field of the Hierarchy. You can enter there only through your heart.

> *Only the heart can unite the consciousnesses separated by centuries.*

A Great One speaks about this, "We had an Initiate Who reincarnated continuously for five or six hundred years. He did great work in politics, education, science, the arts, economy, religion, and philosophy in every incarnation. Once I was walking on a European street when the man suddenly came and hugged Me. He recognized Me, but his mind didn't tell him Who I was and what his contact with Me was. His contact was achieved only through the heart."

We have met many people in our past lives; we built bonds of heart, and sometimes we destroyed bridges between us in various ways and for various reasons. We united and separated and eventually we became parts of a group — a family unit, group, or nation.

A group is an accumulation of people who have built the bonds of heart. In every group there are also those who have built a certain degree of heart unity, but still they have not solved past problems which separated them. Hence, occasional clashes between members.

Clashing people must realize that they should work on their differences and problems in order to build stronger bonds of heart. They must control their personality reactions and approach each other through their hearts.

Once a person is a member of a group, he must try to cultivate unity by sacrificing all those elements that separate him from others. If this is not done, life will bring conflicting parties, or individuals, together and force them to build, or destroy, the bonds of heart.

Life gives opportunities, but it does not decide the course to be taken. Thus, a group is an accumulation of hearts that, to a lesser or greater degree, build bonds of heart between each other.

Those who cannot adapt themselves to the group for personality reasons are those who cannot yet overcome past wounds caused by certain members. These wounds hurt and irritate them. However, bonds with other members draw them to the group, or the group leader.

Again, such a person must try to overcome his personalty reactions and try, by all means, to build bonds of heart, overcoming his pride, arrogance, vanity, and ego which were built in the past as protective measures during moments of clashes and separatism.

When a person becomes a member of a group, he must do all that is possible to conquer his personalty defects and cultivate his heart qualities.

To be a member of a group does not mean to pass through a ritual or to sign a paper. It means to accept the spiritual principles that are the goals of the group. Those who accept such principles are members.

One can cultivate his heart by understanding all the above principles. A person can also cultivate his heart by controlling his arrogance, slander, ego, vanity, and pride until they are annihilated in the love of his heart that is felt toward other people.

In every incarnation we have an opportunity to renew the bonds of our heart, or to destroy the bridges built in the past.

The Decaying Heart

In the Ageless Wisdom, there are many references to the concept that one must follow his heart. We read in *Heart,* for example:

> ...*It is precisely the quality of the magnet that is inherent in the heart. The highest creativeness is imbued with this great law. Hence, each consummation, each union, each great cosmic unification is achieved through the flame of the heart....*[1]

We have three main channels of communication with our environment. The first one is the head or

---

1.　Agni Yoga Society, *Heart,* para.1.

the mind. The second is the solar plexus. The third is the heart.

The solar plexus is the center of instinct and emotions. Many people communicate through the solar plexus. Others communicate through their mind, but relatively few communicate through their heart. Communication through the solar plexus, or instinct, is related to natural phenomena, for example, instinctive awareness that rain will fall, lightening will hit, winds will blow, weather will change, earthquakes, fires, and typhoons will occur, etc. The instinct, or solar plexus, also registers the sex drives and urges of others. It leads people to food sources. Instinct causes people to feel the physical and emotional states of family members and group members.

The solar plexus acts as a mind in average people, and with various negative emotions it controls their lives. The solar plexus also registers the magnetic and electrical currents and builds the mood of the person, his inclinations and choices. Most of the time, even above average people fall under the control of their solar plexus when waves of anger, fear, hatred, jealousy, and revenge hit them.

Mental communication enables a person to utilize Nature for self-interest. Through the mind, such a person is able to harness the energies and forces of Nature and use them to meet needs such as food, shelter, and clothing. He also uses these energies and forces to manipulate and exploit others to increase his own prosperity and luxury. All mental communication is based on self-satisfaction and self-interest at individual, group, and national levels if the mind is not led by the heart.

If the mind follows the lead of the solar plexus and is used to satisfy the cravings of the solar plexus, then the mind creates those situations which eventually trap others and lead them into actions that are anti-survival. The mind becomes the trap, as is the case at present, for all humanity. Those who *see* the failure of their mind, resign from the methods they were using and seek refuge in the heart.

Humanity has created all of the current poisons, pollution, radioactivity, insecticides, war machines, nuclear weapons, and chemical and germ warfare. This has restricted human relations in such a way that no lasting peace, understanding, freedom, and joy will be possible. Humanity has trapped itself and does not know how to escape from the trap.

We know clearly that pollution is killing the planet, but thus far we have not been able to stop it. To stop pollution would hurt millions of people economically. People prefer to die slowly and still receive their paychecks.

Heart communication is related to motives, intentions, all-inclusiveness, unity, synthesis, understanding, consciousness, compassion, and right human relations. Such a communication is immediate, direct, and intuitive. It sees the cause before the result manifests.

The human soul is the synthesizer of these three centers — the heart, mind, and solar plexus. If the human soul is able to unify these three channels and bring them together as one device of communication, he enters into the path of perfection.

The majority of people communicate through their solar plexus regardless of their level of education or social position. The solar plexus controls their lives. It is possible to have a great amount of knowledge but still be controlled by the solar plexus. It is sometimes possible to unite the solar plexus and mental channels. In such a case, the mind uses the animalistic urges and drives of man to satisfy its instincts. It also uses jealousy and hatred, or falls into vanity, separativeness, and ego trips.

It is also possible to fuse the solar plexus and the heart, but this creates great difficulties between instincts and Intuition. Eventually, human beings must fuse these three centers, and make the heart the dominating factor in their lives. It is the human soul who brings these three centers together and creates integration and wholeness in man.

Often, these three centers work one at a time. As the evolution of a person develops, two of them act together, and in some cases the three centers function together. This is the moment when man has become conscious and has expanded his consciousness.

The heart center has twelve sensitive petals which record twelve feelings of the heart — the twelve virtues. The *heart* is the fountain of all beauty, love, and compassion which makes life an experience of joy, freedom, and creativity — if your solar plexus and mind do not interfere with the way the heart operates.

Many thoughts or ways of thinking, memories, and plans of the mind interfere with the heart. Many negative emotions disturb the heart, and the person cannot hear the message that the heart wants to give. The mind demands proof, and the solar plexus creates excitement. The heart does not work with forces of excitement. The heart is intuitive and sees the causes long before the results appear on the surface. The heart works in deep peace, and if fused with the solar plexus and mind, it uses them as carriers of its messages of love and clear thinking without illusion, ego, glamor, and separativeness.

Conversely, when the solar plexus and the mind steal light from the heart, they distort and encapsulate it, using it for the self, for separative interests, for their self-image, and for the imposition of their will on others. Such behavior works against your heart, against your own survival, against your prosperity, health, and happiness.

To liberate yourself from such a situation, you are going to make an effort to come in contact with your heart and, in its light, see exactly what you are through your Intuition and compassion.

To be in tune with the heart means to be extremely sincere with yourself and see if there is any trace of self-deception. Once you stand in the light of your heart, you can very clearly see your behavior, your motives and direction, and realize the damage you are doing to your future. By doing this, there is a possibility that you can save your future.

A decaying heart is a reality. The petals of the heart center, as sensitive receivers of higher impressions, can petrify and lose their sensitivity, like a dying flower that loses its vitality, color, and beauty. Once the heart becomes insensitive to higher impressions, it turns into a center of negative emotions such as fear, anger, hate, jealousy, revenge, treason, slander, malice, and greed. Such a center works against the survival of a person. It darkens the path of his future and makes the human organism fall prey to germs, microbes, and viruses.

A decaying heart turns into a center of negative emotions which are usually used for destructive purposes. Some people think that negative emotions can be used constructively and in beneficial ways. Of course, even poison can be used to destroy certain microbes. But, if possible, why not use positive emotions with more highly constructive results. Instead of hate, you can use love, compassion, and sympathy — which make a deeper impression. When you hate someone, you cannot see possibilities in him. You only want to destroy him. What would happen if he gained the power to destroy you?

You might ask, "But we must hate crime, war, destruction, etc." Do you really need to hate crime and war to annihilate them? Can't you see what they do? Can't you use your common sense and reason to stop them? In hating war, you hate those who play war games. Does your hatred produce peaceful solutions, or does it make people more aggressive and hateful toward you?

Negative emotions dull your consciousness, logic, and reasoning so that eventually you turn into an animal rushing toward your victims without calculating the possible reaction and result of the clash. However, positive emotions such as love, enthusiasm, goodwill, peacefulness, fearlessness, and compassion create conditions in which your

Intuition, mind, reason, logic, and heart work to their maximum capacity. They help you solve your problems and the problems of others constructively and for mutual benefit.

A blooming heart can take firm action against corruption, decay of character, insanity, stupidity, and exploitation, but without hate. Hate makes you duplicate and attract to yourself things that you hate.

To be emotional about destructive things, to be emotional about situations in which you feel you cannot do anything, is not a negative attitude. Often the world conditions affect us so deeply that we sit and cry. But such emotional excitement must be used as a source of energy to put your practical plans into action and to correct bad conditions in the world.

Emotions are great sources of energy if they are altruistic, inclusive, and on the line of aspiration and striving. Positive emotions are intuitive currents which carry with them the high voltage of enthusiasm, courage, daring, and fearlessness. Positive emotions sustain and nourish our devotion and dedication. Positive emotions provide fiery vehicles for our thoughts and energy for our actions.

The source of positive emotions is endless. Positive emotions eventually turn into enthusiasm and into Divine Fire which annihilate all kinds of obstacles on the path of our vision.

A decaying heart means you are working against your own survival, since the heart is the center of life and survival.

To let your heart decay in order to gain short range benefits works against your own prosperity and future.

You must try not to relate to people only through your mind and through your solar plexus; use your heart, too. First, try to see yourself as you are; then look at the situation very clearly with an intuitive and compassionate manner, but not in order to save your own face. If there is any deception in your heart, you are not tuned to the right station. By tuning to the right station, you can expand your consciousness and eventually become a super-human being. This happens when you really start facing yourself in your heart and start seeing exactly what you are and what you are doing within the three worlds of your personality.

To unfold your heart further, take each of the following virtues and meditate daily for ten minutes upon their deeper meanings. Visualize yourself as if you were actualizing such virtues in your life. It is very uplifting also to remember those people in history who have demonstrated such virtues.

There are many levels of virtues. We have virtues of Initiates, disciples, aspirants, and average persons. There are virtues which are related to our Spiritual Triad, others to the twelve-petaled Chalice in the higher mental plane. There are other virtues that are radiations of the lotus of the heart.

All these virtues have one common denominator. They all lead the pilgrim toward the direction of the Cosmic Magnet through gradual and continuous transmutation, transformation, and transfiguration.

Let us discuss some of the virtues:

1. Pure motives

2. Striving

3. Sincerity

4. Enthusiasm

5. Responsibility

6. Devotion

7. Dedication

8. Purity

9. Inclusiveness

10. Synthesis

11. Identification

12. Sacrificial service

13. Patience

14. Wisdom

15. Nobility

You can take this list and meditate on one virtue every day.

Pure motives. Daily try to have pure, selfless motives behind all your mental, emotional, and physical actions. Examine your motives and if they are not harmless, pure, and are not selfless, throw them out and import new and higher motives. Higher motives help you externalize your True Self.

There may be conflicts between your heart and mind. The mind tries to conceal its motives. The heart reveals the motives, but sometimes it does not win. Nevertheless, the truth remains in the chamber of the heart. The heart registers everything that the solar plexus and mind do, but it is often too weak to take the lead.

People rush to criticize and measure and judge others. But, the most important thing is to catch yourself and see if your motives are right. The heart tells you, if that heart is purified of interference by the solar plexus and the mind. You need the mind and the solar plexus **if they are under the light and guidance of the heart.** Your intellect, your mind, is going to be the servant of the heart if you are going to step on the path of perfection, on the path of sincerity, on the path of becoming a human being.

The solar plexus is a very important center also. It has two parts, lower and higher. The higher part, if unfolded, is used for psychic healing. The lower part registers all lower psychic conditions going on in its environment. If this lower part is out of control, it can take its owner to the asylum.

If you are focused primarily in the lower part of the solar plexus, you are half animal. If you are totally mental, you are a satan, which is worse than being an animal. If you have a scientific mind that is totally dedicated to self-interest, ego, and vanity, it is satan itself.

You must be able to feel and see the motives of people — people appear in many sheepskins. Christ talked about this.

There are many examples of sheepskins:

"I am very honest."

"I am fulfilling my responsibilities."

"I am dedicated and sacrificial."

"I am truthful."

"I am doing everything possible to do everything possible."

Do not deceive yourself and do not let other people deceive you. When you really turn to the center of your heart, you can suddenly see in the mirror, in the center of your heart, the real image. Until you come to this focus, you are not a useful human being. Instead, you are a person who creates disturbances, distortions, and various complications. You turn into a self-interested viper in life.

Striving is the result of the divine pressure within the chalice. This pressure urges you to unfold, achieve, and accomplish great service for humanity. It is interesting that the heart is the source of striving which, with the cooperation of mind, leads the human soul to higher achievements.

If the mind is left alone, it creates those conditions in which you slowly become encased in inertia, apathy, pleasures, luxury, etc. You forget the rest of life. This is a very dangerous situation which develops slowly, so slowly that you cannot feel that you are facing grave danger.

When you have trouble, stick to your heart and strive. To strive means to go against the mechanical currents of life that are taking all of us away from our divine destiny.

Sincerity is another virtue. If we do not develop sincerity from top to bottom, there is no hope for us. In the New Testament, Christ placed the greatest emphasis on the dangers of hypocrisy. You make yourself appear to be something, but in your heart you are not exactly what you appear to be. Hypocrisy is dangerous because it disturbs your real image and creates second, third, and fourth personalities. You start acting as multiple persons. Eventually, you become so many different persons you lose the real one. You ask, "Who am I?" You start searching for the real one you were. This is a very catastrophic and deplorable situation. Sometimes people think that they are not in such a situation, but they are really in it. They have so many images in their mind, and so many images that others have built about them which they import. Eventually, they do not know which image they are.

Once a man said to me, "The reason I drink is to find who I am."

"The reason you drink is that you want to forget all those personalities that you are identified with," I answered.

Enthusiasm is a very powerful virtue emanating from the heart. Only the heart has enthusiasm, not the solar plexus, nor the mind. People sometimes mistake enthusiasm for excitement. They say, "Look at this woman and man doing everything, running everything, and jumping into everything." This is excitement. It is an effort to release the agitations they have in their nature. It is not enthusiasm. Enthusiasm is called the Divine Fire. In enthusiasm, all of your actions, thoughts, and emotions are related to the Divine Plan and the Divine Intent and the Divine Purpose. In that case, you know that you do not know everything, and you do not do anything unless you are tuned to the Highest Center within the Planet. Enthusiasm is to bring Beauty, Goodness, Righteousness, Joy, Freedom, and sincerity into expression through your sacrificial labor.

Those who want to have such virtues must go through very hard times and through great difficulties until all of the obstacles and "monkeys" that dwell in their mind and solar plexus are thrown out. You must allow teachers, your leaders, or your priests to help you to crush these things in your nature. If you are not allowing them to be crushed, there is no hope for you. You will stay in that heavily guarded and covered grave.

The fifth virtue is *responsibility*. The heart is always responsible. When you see things occurring, you can immediately see if there is responsibility or irresponsibility behind them. An irresponsible person does things half way. Irresponsible persons complicate situations which cannot be solved. Such people are called "I know everything and I can do everything" people. When you give such people a job to do, they really create chaos in the job as well as create chaos in you because they are irresponsible.

To be responsible means to know and to do exactly what you know how to do, and to do exactly what is needed from you. If you do not know, do not do the job because in doing so you destroy your own image, the image of others, and the work. Eventually, you fall into apathy and guilt feelings.

When one shows respect for his duties and responsibilities, we say, "This person is really receiving energy from a higher petal of the heart." Each petal is an electronic tube which puts you in communication with Higher Realms.

Heartlessness develops in man when he avoids his responsibilities. We are told that the heart cannot be cultivated unless a person meets his responsibilities.

Devotion is the next virtue. Devotion is steady service to the highest degree possible. There is no devotion if you are giving all your energy and resources to hurt and exploit people and gratify your ego and vanity.

Devotion is directed to an ideal. Devotion gives, sacrifices, and does not expect self-interest.

You are going to devote yourself. Devotion is putting yourself into a job, into a cause, into a purpose, to create better conditions in the world.

Dedication is another virtue. In dedication, you start using your mind for your purpose and making your mind an instrument of your heart. Your heart says, "Mind, this is the correct path." The mind screams and says, "What if I like this, this, and this?" "What about me?" "What about my family?" "What about my situation, my positions, my income?" The heart says, "There are other ways to be happy and to be fulfilled." Do you find yourself in the situation where your mind fights against your heart? Which one wins? If your heart is winning, you are making a contact with the mind and putting your mind under the control of your heart. You are making your mind dedicate itself to the heart and the purpose of the heart.

Purity is another virtue of the heart. Purity is thoughts, actions, and feelings that are in tune with the heart. Every time you are against the heart, you are impure. Every time you are with the heart, you are pure, regardless of what people might say. When you are with your mind and its criticisms, its measuring and judgments, you are always wrong; you are always polluted. **Only the heart has the keynote of your life.** If you lose this keynote, all of your life will be built on the wrong foundation.

Inclusiveness. Often when we speak about inclusiveness, people think about a *trash can*. Many people think that inclusiveness means to bring sheep and wolves together and let them eat each other. They think that inclusiveness is a trash can in which you put the jewels, the garbage, etc. But real inclusiveness means to disperse, reject, and avoid everything that works against love and compassion, against unity and synthesis.

Synthesis is a great virtue. If you develop such a virtue you will see the causes of events, the causes of the behaviors of others, and you can forecast future events. Synthesis enables you to relate many factors and see the forces behind them.

Synthesis exists in Nature. The heart realizes it and tries to make men live non-separative lives.

Those who develop synthesis eventually see clearly how things are related to each other.

Identification is another virtue of the heart. The heart identifies with those who are happy and with those who are unhappy, and through identification one discovers the true reasons why happiness or unhappiness, joy or sorrow exist.

Identification develops compassion. Gradually this virtue develops to such a degree that it turns into a source of information, wisdom, and power.

Sacrificial service is one of the great virtues of an unfolding heart.

Sacrificial service can be defined as mental, emotional, and physical actions that bring definite changes in your environment, causing transformation and change of consciousness.

With your thoughts, words, and actions, you become a transmitter of the transforming energy of your innermost Core. Your environment, people related to you, their psychology, consciousness, and directions change toward living a life of Beauty, Goodness, Righteousness, Joy, and Freedom.

Sacrificial service is not intended to force, to impose, or to violate the freedoms of others in any degree, in any way, but to create a transformative influence by which people are enthused to change themselves and their lives.

Sacrificial service can be rendered by renouncing certain possessions, by keeping silent, by having a selfless attitude, by inspiring and challenging people, by working hard and removing the obstacles in people's way, by discovering wisdom and offering it to others, by being indifferent to praise and insult, by doing hard work to illuminate people...irrespective of their attitudes.

Not everyone can render a sacrificial service. To be able to, one needs a great amount of flow of willpower and at least an intuitional contact with its source.

Sacrificial service is related to the innermost Core of the human being. When the current of this Core releases itself to activate the mental, emotional, and physical bodies into labor, we say that the person is engaged in sacrificial service. What this means is that with every action on any plane, the server brings transformation and releases the Divinity in those who are related to him. Servers act as transmitters of divine energy without any personal expectation of glory or interest.

Sacrificial service burns away all accumulations of egoism and paves the way for inclusiveness, unity, and renunciation of the personal self.

Sacrificial service dissipates all illusions, glamors, and maya, which serve as hotbeds for the germs of egoism.

Sacrificial service destroys all thoughtforms, feelings, and actions based on separatism.

Patience is a great virtue. We read in the Teaching:

> *In upward flights we learn the great gift*
> *of patience. Radiant, creative patience*
> *does not resemble the murky cloak of non-*
> *resistance to evil.... Creative patience*
> *holds the key to the New World; therefore,*

> *patience creates a power which is inten-*
> *sified with each hour of reality.*[2]

Also,

> *Without a realization of patience it is im-*
> *possible to reflect on Infinity. The dimen-*
> *sions of the tasks of the Higher World*
> *require tests of patience.*[3]

One of the greatest benefits from patience is that it eliminates the possibility of irritation and the deadly poison created by irritation.

In the future, people will understand that the cause of the various kinds of heart disease is irritation. Patience avoids such a source of suffering.

Patience also clarifies the mind and makes it work with the Intuition of the heart.

Patience creates a protective net around the heart.

Wisdom is understood as the Holy Spirit, the primordial Light which exists in every atom, in every form, in every man, and in every living form beyond man.

This is the "wisdom from above" to which St. James refers.

He refers also to another kind of wisdom which he calls "terrestrial, devilish wisdom."[4]

2.   Agni Yoga Society, *Community*, para. 162.
3.   Agni Yoga Society, *Aum*, para. 244.
4.   James 3:15

The true wisdom is gained by a person in absorbing the primordial Light, the Holy Spirit, into his heart.

We are told that this Light is contacted consciously when a person purifies himself — his threefold inner nature — and penetrates into the Intuitional Plane through his heart. The primordial Light is then contacted and appropriated by the purified heart and mind and made applicable in solving the problems of life.

Love is one of the components of wisdom, the other being intelligence, fused together in the flame of the heart.

Wisdom handles all problems in the light of love and pure logic, in the light of harmlessness and practicality, and in harmony with the Holy Spirit existent in the whole Universe.

The terrestrial wisdom is knowledge and experience collected throughout ages in the mental plane like a bank. All knowledge collected and experience gathered cannot be called "devilish" or terrestrial. It is only one factor which makes that wisdom "devilish" and that factor is the "egoism" — the vanity, self-interest, and separatism in one package. It is the ego that uses the treasury of knowledge and experience for selfish reasons, exploitation, manipulation, and slavery. This is how wisdom becomes "devilish."

If you use your wisdom to create crimes, manipulate people and nations, exploit their resources, emotions, and ignorance, you prove that you have wisdom, but a "devilish" wisdom.

"Devilish" wisdom can also be drawn from those entities who serve dark forces. They have stores of "terrestrial" wisdom of thousands of ages, and if they find a ready channel, they give him "wisdom" to carry their destructive plans on earth.

Divine wisdom increasingly shines within those who approach the flame of their heart. You can see the wisdom increasing in those who put their feet on the Path, and gradually become true aspirants, disciples, Initiates, Arhats, Masters, Chohans, and Resurrected Ones.

Beyond them you can see the Angelic Kingdom, charged with the light of wisdom, which transmits it to those who are in tune with the Cosmic Heart.

This wisdom is sometimes called the "hidden wisdom" that can be imparted only to those who are on the path of perfection.

To acquire wisdom we are told there are five steps:

1. Purification of the threefold nature of man

2. Education

3. Meditation

4. Labor, sacrificial service

5. Inclusiveness

It is through these five main steps that one readies himself to absorb wisdom, grow in wisdom, and serve in wisdom.

Whenever wisdom is in action, you can be the radiation of the five-pointed star of Beauty, Goodness, Righteousness, Joy, and Freedom. These are the fruits of wisdom to which St. James referred in his Epistle.

Wisdom is present everywhere, but one must make himself ready with the above steps to absorb and be charged with it.

Every pure heart is a chalice of wisdom.

Wisdom has two levels: theoretical and real. Theoretical wisdom can include wisdom from books, from other people, from observing life events. If such wisdom has no virtue behind it, it turns into a science of manipulation. There are wise people in every department of human endeavor who can easily manipulate millions of people.

There are many politicians, educators, scientists, religious leaders, financiers, and others who have wisdom, but their wisdom is *earthly* not "heavenly."

The second and true wisdom comes from a deep analysis of the effects and causes of many experiences. It is the realization of a spiritual principle which uses such an analysis or such a conclusion for creative ends, in harmony with the progressive currents of life. This is wisdom from heaven.

The first wisdom is not the wisdom referred to by the disciples of wisdom. Of course, such a wisdom is also not easy to acquire. For example, it takes one hundred years or many lives to learn how to manipulate people for your own or your national interests. This sort of wisdom needs the accumulation of a vast amount of experience. But, in itself, it has no higher purpose or higher value; it is earthbound.

On the other hand, the heavenly wisdom has measures, principles, virtues, as well as experience and intellect which are used to help the creative forces in Nature bring about a better world — one that is economically prosperous, psychologically cooperative and peaceful, mentally progressive and expanding, and spiritually in tune with Higher Worlds.

Schools of wisdom must be reestablished everywhere in the world, as they were ten thousand and fifteen thousand years ago, teaching the science of living on earth and the science of contacting the Higher Worlds.

The schools of wisdom in the future will teach us how to use our experience to call forth the innermost potential found in every man and annihilate the barriers between the lower and the subjective or Higher Worlds.

The Kingdom of God is a state of consciousness in which wisdom creates harmony between all that is on earth and all that is in "heaven."

Nobility is another virtue. Nobility is respect for yourself and others. Nobility is the ability to recognize the limits, the borders of the mental, emotional, and physical bodies and the duties and responsibilities in which you are living. It is knowing where you are going and how you must not go out of your limits. Nobility means always to live in the presence of the compassion and light of your heart.

Nobility is the realization of your inherent Divinity. If you live a life according to that realization, you are a noble soul. It is your innate Divinity that shines through all your thoughts, emotions, words, and actions. That inner Divine Presence is the cause of all striving, patience, persistence, and nobility.[5]

A noble person radiates many virtues through all his relationships. Nobility gives him charm, magnetism, and charisma.

Nobility builds a shield around the person and protects him from the arrows of heartless people.

Nobility awakens in others a striving toward nobility.

The greatest calamity in life is the decay of the heart. Increasing crime, violence, license, murder in movies, literature, and in actual life are signs of decaying hearts.

Never let your heart decay, and never be the cause of any act that decays the hearts of others.

When the heart decays, the psychic energy slowly departs, and the heart goes through a petrification process. All virtues vanish one by one, leaving the person a vacant and ruined house.

How Does the Heart Decay?

The first thing that petrifies the heart is harmful actions, harmful thinking, harmful words, and harmful directions. When you are in harmful conditions, and when you are harming things such as Beauty, Goodness, Truth, men, women, children,

---

5. For further information about Nobility, please refer to *Psyche and Psychism*, Chapter 110, "Nobility."

your job, groups, plans, etc., your heart petals start drooping. Crime does this. Vivisection does it. Hatred does it. Violence does it. Above all, guilt feelings cause the petals to droop. When you feel more and more guilty, your heart closes because you created that situation and you are not worthy to have an open heart. You are going to be very watchful not to do anything that would cause the heart petals to droop or anything that would disturb the balance and unfoldment of the heart.

The heart closes with thoughts, feelings, and actions that are based on malice, slander, and separatism. Separatism leads you into crimes, into destruction and violence, and into guilt. It is so deep, but scientifically and historically you must see what happens. When the heart of a group is closed, that group becomes criminal. If a nation's heart is destroyed, it becomes aggressive, destructive, and separative. If a father's heart is closed, it is very painful for children to have such a father. Be careful, and see that your heart is guarded.

Hatred and revengefulness destroy your heart. Maybe one hundred years from now, geniuses will show on television the petals of the heart and demonstrate how anger causes the petals to droop, dry, and fall.

Jealousy is very bad for your heart. Sometimes heart disease comes when, in one or another instance, you work against the flame of the heart. You must be very careful. If you cause one of the petals to dry or atrophy, it takes many, many years to repair. King Solomon said, "Guard the temple of your heart." Do not do anything against your heart.

The heart is pure Intuition, and it sees everything as it is.

Ugliness destroys the heart — ugly clothes, ugly make-up, ugly behavior, ugly relationships, ugly films, etc. If you observe these things scientifically and psychologically, you will see how ugliness works against your survival. If you show ugly films to five beautiful children, one year later they will be failing, to some degree, in their classes. People living in beautiful environments are more wholesome than those who live in ugly and polluted cities.

Exploitation and manipulation really close the heart. Do not engage in these activities; you will pay for them later. Let us say that you have closed four or five petals. You will need at least five incarnations of suffering to repair the damage. You might say, "I am finished with it. I escaped." Why are millions of children being born with handicaps? M.M. says, "Go to the hospitals, especially children's hospitals, and observe. This is a good way for you to know what karma does." It is very sobering. You will see millions of paralyzed and mentally retarded children in addition to many children with various physical defects. This is the result of how they lived in the past.

You may say, "I gossiped and slandered and did many other bad things, but nothing happened." Again, you are gliding on the surface. Wait! The Computer, **Karma**, is at work, and in due time your bill will come due.

Cruelty is very bad for your heart petals. You beat your children and scold them. This creates a bad image in them. Then you attack and curse your wife or husband. You do cruel things to others that make them cry and tremble and lose hope for the future.

Cruel action also means not to do your duties and responsibilities as they should be done. This is cruelty because you are stealing the time and money of others, and preventing others from doing the work better than you. Watch these things. They are told to you with great compassion, so that you can escape from the trap you are creating for yourself.

One starts cruelty gradually. First you kill a bug, then a lizard, followed by a fox, a sheep, and an ox. Next you begin hurting, harming, and being cruel to human beings, and a time comes when you can kill armies or a nation without feeling the slightest pain in your heart. This is when your heart is sold to Satan. This pattern shows the steady and gradual drooping of the heart petals. The heart center loses all of the micro-links which tie a person to the currents of Compassion and the All-existing Spark of God, and the flame in your heart exists no more.

Treason is a poison for the heart. There is no greater sin than treason. But when the heart is really healthy, you have God within you, and you do not fall into the pit of treason.

Q&A

Question: *Can you explain the meanings of guilt and compassion?*

Answer: Compassion is unconditional dedication to the human welfare. Guilt is the result of satisfying your own desires in legal and in illegal ways. When people try to satisfy their vanities and desires at the expense of the joy, happiness, and freedom of others, they feel very guilty. Compassion is total dedication and devotion to the human welfare. Regardless of how people crucify the compassionate one or burn him at the stake, he will say, "I will still serve humanity."

> **Question:** *Can you pay your karma and still be in your heart, and can you pay the karma without waiting for several years?*

Answer: You do not create karma if you live in the flame of your heart because you never do anything against the Law of Love and Compassion. Love and compassion are fires in the heart. If you are in the heart, you will never have karma.

But how can we erase our past karma? We do this by trying very sincerely and eagerly to live a life of harmlessness. This minimizes our karma.

Let us say that you are a millionaire sitting on your sofa and saying, "Thank God, I finally did it! I am very happy." Then, at some point, you want to enter into your heart. Your heart will say, "Whatever you have collected, share with others and follow me." Christ told about this in the story of the wealthy man who came to Him. The man asked how he could enter into the kingdom of God. Christ told him that he was very beautiful, but the one thing he needed to do was to share everything he owned and follow Him. The man was silent and left. Christ said, "It is so difficult to reach people who are tied and say, 'My jewels, my nation, my property, my this, my that.' " The heart screams and cries, but there is no way for such people to enter into the heart.

Karma can be cleared by distributing the wealth to others which you accumulated for your own self. This is why the wealthy man escaped. Christ said, "He is so beautiful, but he can't do it." That man was going to be a disciple. What would have happened if he had become a disciple? If he had become a disciple that day, he was going to be with Christ for two thousand years. To be with the Highest Consciousness on this planet means to have all the opportunities to bloom into Divinity. He lost that because he had five acres, or five million dollars, or five girl friends, etc. He could not leave them behind.

Question: *Can you expand on the concept of identification?*

Answer: To identify means to feel one with others. When a child is crying, you become one with that child and say, "I know why you are crying." When a person is failing, you do not laugh and enjoy his failure. You do not enjoy his manipulation, his exploitation, his various tricks and ways to cheat people. You cry in your heart, and you identify with him and feel his guilt because the guilt of everyone is your own guilt.

Question: *What steps can we take to guard our heart?*

Answer: Follow the twelve virtues of the heart as presented in this book and in *The Psyche and Psychism*.[6] Meditate on them, and practice them. It will slowly clean the paths and jungles and lead you into the heart.

It is not easy to enter into the heart. It needs very hard work, self-examination, confrontation with yourself and with your past, then resignation: "God, I renounce all of these stupid things I have been doing. Now I am at Your disposal." If you do this, you can enter into the heart. We are going to do this if we can, but we must go slowly but not lose time.

> **Question:** *You once gave an example of a man who committed a crime with one of his arms. Then, the Teacher had him do good things with the same arm to clean his karma.*

Answer: The things collected must be gathered and shared. It is just like incurring a debt. You owe several dollars to this and that person, and some to your mortgage, etc. You slowly lose your head because you are under your karma.

The best way is to work very hard to be spiritually wealthy and pay off your creditors. But if you do not pay, they will come and *squeeze* it from you. "As above, so below." In Higher Worlds and lower worlds, the law is the same but at different levels.

---

6. *The Psyche and Psychism*, Vol. II, Chapters 92-107.

Question: *I experienced a wonderful ac-*
complishment. At first I felt that I
shouldn't be happy about it and should
hide it. Then I decided to go ahead and
enjoy it and became excited about the ac-
complishment. How can I tell the dif-
ference between the vanity of the
accomplishment and the real joy?

Answer: The answer for me is joy. First, you
measured things with the solar plexus. The solar
plexus made you very happy with what you did,
and you started developing vanity and pride, etc.
Then, the solar plexus stopped and the mind began
with, "You are a great man. You did such a beautiful
thing." This greatly exaggerated your accomplishment. You lose your balance and economy with the
mind and start believing that you are the only one
who can do good things. This is against the heart.

The heart rejoices without personal interest,
vanity, ego, or showing off when you do something
good. It is pure joy. Even if people praise you, it does
not matter. Neither praise nor criticism can disturb
you because your heart is in joy.

The present situation of the world can change if
humanity subordinates its solar plexus and mind to
its heart. The heart is the carrier of the Torch of
Universal Brotherhood and Universal Peace.

The liberation of a human being is achieved
through an unfolding heart. The liberation of
humanity is achieved through living according to
the virtues of the heart.

The future education will be dedicated to the education of the heart.

The greatest benefactors of the human race are those who had and have flaming, all-inclusive hearts.

> *The most wondrous fire is the flame of the heart saturated with love for Hierarchy.*[7]

---

7.   Agni Yoga Society, *Hierarchy*, para. 352.

The Heart and
Other Worlds

> ...the Teaching of the Heart is so needed
> for the life of the future. Otherwise how
> will you cross the boundaries of the
> worlds?[1]

One crosses the Other Worlds through an un-folding heart.[2]

People of encyclopedic knowledge and of higher positions remain in the lower strata of the world unless their heart is aflame.

---

1. Agni Yoga Society, *Heart*, para. 388.
2. For full information on this subject of Higher Worlds, see *Other Worlds*.

The "boundaries of the worlds" is an expression which refers to the planes of existence, the various dimensions through which man must pass to come in contact with a more abundant life.

The Teaching of the Heart will prepare humanity to advance toward future possibilities.

Without the Teaching of the Heart, humanity will exterminate itself. It is important that the leaders of the world prepare the Teaching of the Heart and spread it all over the world as the foundation of right human relations, goodwill, harmony, cooperation, sense of responsibility, unity, and synthesis.

It is possible that in cultivating the hearts of the people of the earth, the leader creates a safe world, a happy and prosperous world, a world without exploitation and crime, a world in which it will be possible to actualize our highest dreams, our highest visions.

It is the Teaching of the Heart that will regenerate the world through the focus of love and compassion and eliminate all kinds of exploitation, manipulation, and fear.

The Teaching of the Heart in the ancient world was called Sun-knowledge. "...In this definition was indicated the fieriness, the sunlike quality, the centrality of the heart...."[3]

It is impossible "to cross the boundaries of the worlds" without being equipped and charged with

---

3. Agni Yoga Society, *Heart*, para. 339.

fire — with Sun — and without focusing within your own center.

Brain knowledge is not a transforming factor. It is not the knowledge that is used for the divine alchemy but the fire of the heart. All transmutation, transformation, and transfiguration processes are carried out within a human being through the fire of the heart. For each world you must develop a new vehicle. This vehicle can be built only by the flame of the heart.

> *...The brain and all the centers are the estates of the heart....*[4]

Contemporary education is limited by the brain, but the brain must be looked at as one of the estates of the heart. When the heart is developed and unfolded, the brain turns into a super computer under the direction of the heart.

There are hidden, secret corners of the brain which can come into action only through the operation of the flame of the heart.

The heart uses all centers to continue its journey toward the Cosmic Heart, crossing world after world through psychic energy, the center of which is within the heart.

> *...The heart is set out like an anchor in a storm....*[5]

---

4. *Ibid.*, para. 339.
5. *Ibid.*, para. 444.

The storm that is devastating the world physically, emotionally, and mentally can be dissolved only through those who carry the torch of their heart.

Inventions of the brain made to destroy, to conquer, to devastate nature and humanity will turn into obsolete mechanisms once our heart directs the activities of our mind.

People try to understand the intentions, the motives, the plans, the secrets of people, but they cannot. Understanding is not the gift of the brain but the power of the heart.

> ...*Whoever shall aid his near ones to find the path of the heart shall also find his own perfection.*[6]

Before you teach science, chemistry, politics, or the arts of war and exploitation, teach people how to find their heart. After the heart is found, the direction of life is found and the purpose of life is seen. Everyone who discovers his heart discovers the source of joy, freedom, beauty, and peace.

By helping others find their heart, you help yourself learn the ways of the heart. It is only through the heart that the ocean of life is crossed and the other shore is discovered.

All dimensions are found in the heart. It is very interesting. The brain talks and eventually you feel dry and thirsty. But talk about the heart is a never

---

6.   *Ibid.*, para. 399.

ending and interesting path. Once the hearts begin to converse with each other, they do not want to stop because layer after layer of new dimensions, new revelations, are unveiled.

People often approach each other with their knowledge, position, possessions, and diplomas but are never able to reach a heart. They do not have the key. The key to the deepest friendship and cooperation is not found in the pockets of brain knowledge, of self-interest, or in money, but in the heart.

The mind swims in vanity, in egoism, in pride, in self-interest, but the heart is sincere, pure, sensitive, all loving, and all inclusive.

Once a little girl said to her father, "You do not have a heart." He was the boss of a big scientific firm. In his hand he had the destiny of hundreds of people, but his daughter knew that he did not have a heart.

"One day you will die and perish like a dry branch, and you will never have life again," said the daughter, and added, "As my father, I want you to discover your heart."

This man was selling chemicals, pesticides, and various other poisons all over the world and spending his money on other women and friends. The daughter knew this. He listened to his daughter's words, and, once when he was in Europe, he found me on a high mountain and told me his story. He asked, "How can I find my heart? My daughter made me lose the game of life. As I hear her voice, I remember all the damage that I have done to millions of people. How can I find my heart?"

I gave him the following verse and said, "Ponder on this verse for one year, and you will find the path leading to your heart."

> Let us accept love as the impetus for the expansion of consciousness. The heart will not be aflame without love; it will not be invincible nor will it be self-sacrificing. Thus, let us give our gratitude to each receptacle of love; it lies on the boundary of the New World, where hate and intolerance are banished. The path of love is the tension of cosmic energy. Thus will people find their place in Cosmos. Not like dry leaves but as flaming lotuses they will be akin to the Highest World.[7]

The man read the verse a few times and asked, "What is a flaming lotus?"

"It is your heart when it unfolds."

He put the paper in his pocket and departed.

As one loves and cares for others, he discovers the path of his heart. As he discovers this path, he discovers not the treasury of knowledge but the treasury of wisdom — which helps him see the purpose of his life, to see the future, to feel the existence of the Other Worlds, and to develop inclusiveness of the heart.

---

7. *Ibid.*, para. 243.

It is the heart that will unite the world. All wisdom is given by great Hearts. Those whom we adore had and have flaming hearts.

> *Not the supernatural, or magic, simply a flaming aspiration of the heart will unite the worlds.*[8]

It is very interesting that in the light of the heart it becomes impossible to hide from our Self. To know oneself, one must increase the light of his heart. Self-knowledge cannot be achieved through knowledge, logic, and reasoning. Such faculties cannot help us reach the Self. The only way to know ourselves is through the path of the heart. If you have heart, you exist. If you have the flame and the light in your heart, you are alive. If you live in your heart, you *know your Self.* Your Self is the key to the door leading to ALL-understanding.

In discovering your heart, you discover the hearts of people. You discover the Divinity in the hearts of people. When Divinity is found, the system of life is found.

It is the flame of the heart which eventually will seal the doors of prisons, the doors of asylums, the doors of hospitals and will stop wars and annihilate the danger of future destructions.

It is deplorable that nations build sanctuaries to glorify their egos and gain superiority over others through their scriptures, prayers, and hymns and

---

8.   *Ibid.,* para. 475.

with ceremonial processions, while their life demonstrates a heartless attitude to neighbors and to the world. The greatest sanctuary in the world is a pure heart, an inclusive heart, a caring heart. If such a sanctuary is not built in the soul of the builders of sanctuaries, the sanctuaries will turn into sources of inspiration for destruction, hatred, separatism, revolutions, and wars.

It is almost the year 2000. We can see that no sanctuary, no religion, no philosophy has been able to stop hatred, exploitation, and wars.

It is only by building the sanctuary of the heart that humanity will see sunny days. Its pain and suffering gradually will disappear because the Temple of the Heart will gather all hearts and lead them to future glories.

Unfold your heart through your prayer, meditation, patience, solemnity, courage and fearlessness, benevolence, purity, love, creativity, beauty, striving, silence, caution, and through the vision of the future. These are the wings of your heart. The whole of Space, with its billions of stars, is waiting for your flight.

❧ The Flame of the Heart

In the heart center of the etheric body there is a blue electric flame which nourishes all our vehicles. This flame must be protected from the disturbances of our mind, emotions, and harmful deeds.

You must guard your heart and not disturb it with mental problems, mental exploitation, hatred, jealousy, malice, slander, anger, irritation, and self-interest. It is the heart that keeps the body really healthy. Very soon the medical profession will discover that the health of the body depends on the purity of the heart. When your heart is pure and the flame is radiating, that Flame of Life burns all that disturbs your being in your physical, emotional, and mental bodies. The Flame, like an electrical energy or fire, slowly permeates these three bodies and purifies them.

Transfiguration is the moment when the flame of the heart enlightens and illuminates every atom in your vehicles. There is a temple within you, the Temple of the Heart. In this temple, there is the Presence of the Most High — which is the Flame. This Flame is your consciousness.

We read in the Psalms, "Create in me, O Lord, a clean heart," and, "O my Lord, renew the right spirit within me." Spirit is the Flame. Create a pure heart and a flame that is straight — not a flickering light. A flickering light bends in every wind, in every emotion, in every temptation, in every test, in every thought. You are going to be a straight flame. We also find in the Bible, "Is there anyone among you who can say, 'I am pure from sin; I have made my heart clean'?" A great Sage says that you die because your heart becomes polluted and eventually gives up. If your heart is kept clean, pure and radioactive, you will be dynamite — so healthy, intelligent, successful, and prosperous. Just a moment's thought will reveal how all your problems — personal problems, family problems, social problems, national and international problems — stem from pollution of the heart. If the heart is pure there are no such problems because it is through the heart that we communicate with each other.

People are mistaken when they think that problems are solved with their mind. If a man has problems with his wife and children and he tries to solve them by using his mind, intellect, and analysis, he will complicate the issues. Try solving problems with the heart and see what happens. If a person

fabricates using logic, reason, diplomacy, and
politics, this will not help at any level from personal
to international. Unless we have people whose
hearts are aflame, we will not find the right direction. The Great Ones do not analyze us or examine
us; They say, "Get up. You are healed!" It is the
heart. Try to dwell in the heart.

Once a person feels the flame in his heart, he
feels the effects throughout his body; his skin comes
alive, something stirs in his bones, and his blood is
new because the flame of his heart transmits three
energies: light, love, and power. The flame of the
heart transmits the Power of the Father, the Love of
the Son, and Holy Spirit, the Mother.

Visualization A

1. Close your eyes and relax.

2. Visualize a golden rose approximately six
   inches behind your shoulder blades. Build
   this rose slowly; do not hurry. See the beautiful golden color and try to imagine the
   twelve petals of that rose.

3. Visualize a blue flame in the center of the
   rose. See it radiating out a pure blue light
   which purifies your whole being — your
   physical, emotional, and mental being.

4. See yourself as a purified and transformed
   human being. All of your anxieties are dis-
   carded, your bodies are energized and

purified, your emotions are calm, and your mind is shining with light.

5. Let the blue flame permeate your being.

6. See the golden rose again with the blue flame at its center, and feel deep joy.

7. At the center of the blue flame, see the image of Christ.

This exercise will improve your sensitivity to the effect of the flame. Once you close your eyes and see the twelve-petaled rose with its central blue flame — a flame which is your Lord — you cannot deceive anymore; you cannot cheat anymore because you realize that at the center of your being there is one thing that exists — the Most High. People think they exist, but who exists except the Most High at the center of their being? If you feel that the Most High exists within your heart, you start living a beautiful life, and out of your heart the living streams that pour forth will regenerate you.

A girl once came to me, depressed, knocked down, and beaten. "I am going to commit suicide," she said. "Well, that is your business if it is what you want to do, but first sit down and close your eyes." I told her to visualize her heart with a flame in it, and to see the flame penetrating into every part of her body. Ten minutes later she began to smile, and she said, "Something has been lifted from me. Something is released." This exercise acknowledges that you and the flame are one. The flame keeps you united with the life principle within you.

In some Eastern books it is written that cancer can be cured through the flame of the heart because this flame is Life.

You have within you a self-generating, self-healing center — God within you. Put it into operation.

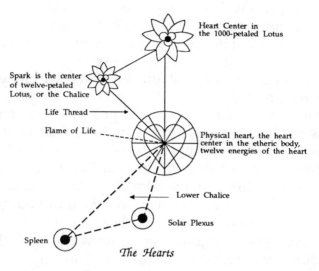

The Hearts

The above diagram is a symbolic presentation of our subtle mechanism. We have here the spleen and solar plexus centers, which together with the heart center form the *minor,* or *lower chalice.* In the core of the heart center there is the *Flame of Life,* radiating twelve virtues which are the carriers of life energy. We also have the *life thread* which bridges the core of the heart with the Spark within the twelve-petaled Lotus in the higher mind. The life thread also bridges the Chalice and the heart center in the head. The Chalice radiates twelve colors corresponding to the twelve virtues in the heart, with red, blue, and yellow as the dominating colors.

Red is Willpower. Blue is Love, or Compassion. Yellow is the Divine Light within you. Translated in Christian terms these are the Father, the Son, and the Holy Spirit within you.

Red, or red-orange, is the power of God within you. If you awaken this power, you will feel that there is nothing that you cannot do. You need this realization. Whatever your profession or school, if you want to help someone but say "I can't," this is the greatest sin against the Presence within you because, as long as the Father is within you, all things are possible. You can be prosperous in business so long as you are going in the right direction. You can build, you can create — **you can** — as long as this flame radiates within you. This flame is the Presence within you, the Almighty Creator in three aspects. Once you feel this power within you, you will never again feel depressed or lonely.

Once you recognize the Father within the other person, you become one with him. The only reason a person sees another as his enemy, or gossips, slanders, and maligns another, is because he does not recognize the Father within the other person who is the same within himself. He does not recognize the flame of the heart.

If you examine the heart of an atom, any atom, you will find that the nucleus is fire. The same is true with a cell. The cells of any living structure have a fiery essence within their core. The emotional and mental planes are built of atoms that have fire within them. Transfiguration and total regeneration occur the moment the central flame releases the fires central to each atom and cell within your bodies —

and you become radioactive. This is the Transfiguration Initiation.

It is written in the Ageless Wisdom that if the
heart leads the mind, it leads to holiness, to perfection, to God. But if the mind leads the heart,
problems are created because the mind is a deceiver
if it does not have the light of the heart. The mind is
always self-centered and self-interested. It is the
heart which leads a man to be interested in the
whole. The heart is inclusive; the mind is separative.
Both are needed to maintain balance. But if the heart
is absent, the mind becomes vicious. In national and
international problems, it is the mind which
deceives, never the heart. The heart knows. Sometimes a person knows he is doing wrong, talking
wrong, or thinking wrong, but his mind rationalizes
and says, "It's okay; go ahead," while his heart says,
"No, it isn't okay; stop." If the person tells his heart
to be quiet, the heart dies and the flame is extinguished. When a person follows his mind, he ends
up in prison. Drug dealers are very intelligent, but
they have no heart.

In the Bible there is a parable about the ten
virgins, five of whom were wise, five of whom were
foolish. The wise ones tended the flame of their
heart; the foolish ones allowed the flame to die.
Those who kept the flame burning met the
Bridegroom and were married in His Joy. The
foolish ones were never united with Him. This
"story" is fact. If the flame of the heart is unlit, you
will be left out. To be left out is very painful. Every
man who does not have a flame in his heart will be
separative, not inclusive, and he will be left out.

The following qualities are present if the red-orange flame of the Father is strong within a person:

1. Decisiveness and perseverance in life. If you lack decisiveness, then you lack the flame. Decisiveness is deciding to become something or to do something, and then following through without faltering until you succeed. Everything that is beautiful must become practical in our lives and not remain abstract so that it has value.

A woman opened a shop and came to see me and asked, "How can I be successful in business?" She would work two days and then take a three-day vacation, so I advised her to cut the vacations and work. "Six hours a day is too much!" she said. I told her, "I work twenty hours a day sometimes, and there is no vacation or time off for holidays. Because I work all the time, I am successful." This is not to say that one does not need a vacation, but there is no need to be stupid. You cannot be successful if you take a vacation every minute, or take a break every two hours for tea and a cigarette, for marijuana, hashish, and other destructive things. What is needed for success is decisiveness and per-severance.

Three young men once came to work under my supervision at a factory. They asked my advice on how to be successful; I told them, "It is very easy. Be decisive and persevering and you will be success-ful." Each of them became a supervisor by practicing decisiveness and perseverance. Do not start a project and then abandon it; finish it. Do not give up when hindrances and obstacles appear. On the contrary, when obstacles and hindrances come our way, they must increase our energy and enthusiasm. This is how we can prove that we have the flame within us.

It is important to remember that the flame is destructive to any obstacle or hindrance. The flame in the heart is destructive to elements which hinder health, happiness, and sanity. In the three levels of the personality, the flame can destroy physical elements, negative emotions, and polluting mental forms, or thoughtforms, motives, and plans. The flame purifies all these forms when it is kindled and nourished.

2. Striving. Striving is a continuous effort to overcome hindrances. In striving we conquer our limitations and hindrances and forge ahead on the path of improvement and perfection.

3. Nobility is the next expression of the flame. Nobility is a state of being a light. Are you really noble in your thoughts, in your relationships, in your reactions and responses? If people insult you or hurt you, do not let it affect you. Remain noble. Sometimes we think, "They are insulting me; I am going to choke them!" Instead, show your beauty. Just radiate beauty and you will conquer them, not by slapping their face, but with the power of your beauty you will knock them down. You must learn to depend on the flame.

4. Honesty. Honesty means not to cheat people; cheating others increases your debt. Be honest because you cannot deceive the flame in the other person. When asked whether or not to pay taxes, Christ said, "Caesar's face is on the coin. Give to Caesar what is Caesar's, and give to God what is God's." Give to God what is due to God; give to earth what is due to earth so that you are honest.

A doctor was having a conversation with me about how much he was enjoying himself by cheating on his wife with four other women. "What kind of enjoyment is that?" I asked him. "You are not being honest with your wife, are you?" He admitted that he was not. "If you are not being honest," I told him, "you are not on the right path, no matter how much enjoyment you are having, whether you are a doctor, a philosopher, or a minister." If a person lacks honesty, he is missing the boat. It is possible to deceive others, but it is impossible to deceive the flame within.

We must overcome the idea that it is possible to fabricate, deceive, mislead, or misuse people. We do this sometimes and we feel very clever, like a man who once told me a story of how he sold a broken-down car to someone. He bragged about how smart he was, how he deceived the man, and how he planned to use the money he made. Two months later he was in a car accident and broke his leg. The whole episode cost him $10,000.

Honesty is a divine law. If you break this law, you suffer the consequences. I have been asked, "Can we be honest in such a world and still survive?" Of course we can. If we do not stick to honesty, we lead the world to corruption.

5. Concentration. When the first flame is strong within a person, he is focused and concentrated in his goal, in his life purpose, in his promises and decisions. If you promise something and then two days later break it without a serious reason, you lack concentration. If you begin a project and then quit before it is complete, you lack concentration. Concentration is a steady, progressive use of energy to reach a particular goal.

6. Action. If the red flame is really ignited within a person, he is a person of action. But the motive and purpose behind the action must be right. If you see a man dying but you do not take action, you are the one who is dead. People stand back and watch their children take drugs, or they let their daughters sleep with many different men without taking action. A man who has this flame in his heart takes wise action. Action does not mean to take a bottle and hit another person over the head. Action in this sense is wise, loving, and beautiful.

7. Power to unite. People are contaminated with the sickness of separatism. It exists everywhere; churches, organizations, groups, nations, and businesses are infested. A man of flame always works to unite, to bring together families, couples, children, groups, and nations. Separatism is a sickness which must not be tolerated. In business, always deal with your co-workers in ways that unite them, using the right foundation. Unity is the right foundation. When you work to unite, you become a beloved son of the Father.

8. Power to renounce and sacrifice. Do you have moments in which you can renounce and sacrifice even your feelings of righteousness and prestige for the sake of peace and unity?

I worked at one time as a supervisor of hundreds of men at a railway station. One day I saw one of the men working hard, but as he worked, he was crying. I asked him what was the matter. "My wife is having trouble; she is pregnant and I do not know who is going to help." "Why are you here?" I asked him. "If I do not work," he replied, "how will I buy bread to take home?" I told him to go home and take care of his wife, and to report to me directly if he had any difficulties. Later he called me from the hospital. "We need ten dollars; can you help?" I sent a messenger with twenty dollars. The baby boy was born, beautiful and healthy; one week later, the man's wife came to me with gratitude and said "Thank you, sir; you saved our lives." The man came to me later, concerned about the amount of time he missed and wanted to know how many days had been cut from his salary. I told him that he would see at the end of the month. His check included three days of overtime pay.

This is how I took care of those laborers — with the heart, not the mind. There were times when I needed workers to stay until midnight; whenever I needed help, the laborers were always there because they knew I loved them. It is not the talking about love, but the application of heart that makes the difference. It is doingness that shows where the heart is.

9. Joyfulness. One of the greatest qualities of the Father, which surprises many people, is joyfulness. Joy is the light of the flame. Many people come home from work and dump all of their problems on the heads of their family members. After a hard day at the office some men come through the door and say, "Give me a beer. Did you hear in the news how that city was destroyed, how the economy has crashed? The world is falling into an abyss. Satan has a hold on everything. The antichrist is everywhere." Instead, why not come home and say, "Hi, everybody! Come, everyone gets a hug!" Or sometimes the husband comes home a little tired and the wife begins to tell him how the children misbehaved, how many windows they broke, that the police came and that they are being taken to court. This is what happens in many homes. But try to remember that joy is the light of the Father.

It is hard to say exactly how many people on earth currently have this flame active in their hearts. It cannot be too great a percentage or we would not have the kinds of political, educational, scientific, economic, and religious crises that exist today. To have a flaming heart is not easy. **Just as the flame of a candle increases at the expense of the candle, selfishness, self-interest, egotism, vanity, and possessiveness must decrease and vanish so that only the flame exists.** This means that a person must be totally purified and transformed, not identified with that which is not real. It is very easy to talk about the flame of the heart, but that flame is going to consume you. Are you ready for this?

When the flame increases, people will dislike you because you are not one of them anymore. If you are working in a nightclub making good money but you start increasing the flame, they will tell you to get lost or fire you because you do not fit in anymore. You will not fit into society because society wants you to cheat, manipulate, exploit, and lie. All of these things are fuel which you will burn and finish. The path of the flaming heart is sometimes a lonely path — lonely for the world, perhaps — but you are with God so you are not really lonely. Angels and Great Ones are always in your company.

There are not many flaming hearts, but many are striving, which is the reason for writing *Challenge For Discipleship*. If a person reads and assimilates this book, he will see the kindling of the flame in his heart.

A disciple has a flaming heart. A disciple is a candle who burns in front of a Great One. Burn, radiate your light, shine your light. Christ put great emphasis on this when He said, "Let your light shine." He did not say we should talk day and night, insulting and separating people. If you let your light shine, people will see it; you will not need to talk about it. If your light is shining, you will be joyful, not depressed; you will not lie or cheat; you will not exploit people. You will not have unclean habits such as using marijuana, alcohol, cigarettes, and the like. You will be industrious. To have this light is not easy because it places a tremendous responsibility upon your shoulders.

If we increase the number of flaming hearts in the world, the world will be totally different. This is

what the disciples of Christ did. They said to Him,
"How will people know that we are Your disciples?
We will not have a certificate or a medallion, and
You did not write anything on our foreheads so that
people will be able to see how great we are because
we were with You." He pitied them and said,
"People will know that you are My disciples if you
demonstrate your love for one another."

There are not many flaming hearts in the world,
but everyone who is sincere must do his best to
increase his light, then let it shine without imposition or fear. Shining the light is a great responsibility. To have light means to live a sacrificial life;
the candle is gone while the flame remains.

A young woman came to my office to tell me
that she was going to Europe with a group to preach
beautiful things. She left, and while there they
preached and sang to spread the gospel. When she
returned, she paid me another visit. "We were so
successful and beautiful." The mood of the conversation changed, however, when I asked her if she
had paid a visit to her parents while she was there.
To my surprise she said, "To hell with them!" She
talked about the love of Jesus but could not find love
for her own parents.

Life is not a masquerade; these are real issues.
You are either going to be real or unreal. To have
this flame means to strive to become real.

To carry the light is not easy, but your light must
shine. You are not going to be a fake carrier. You
must be tested. The greatest test is to suffer for
something in which you believe. If you cannot suffer
for your belief, then you do not have faith in your

belief or in yourself. If you love someone, you will suffer for him. How can you say, "I love you," and then refuse to suffer for that person? The candle symbolically demonstrates how we keep our light lit by "burning" ourselves.

The degree of our greatness is equal to the degree in which we can suffer for others. If we cannot suffer for others, we have no value. Greatness does not come from the amount of a person's wealth, his position, possessions, or title. Only suffering makes a person great. Every Great One suffered because He committed Himself to something very great. It is not the suffering that comes from taking LSD and then having horrible hallucinations until it wears off.

Suffering is not self-pity. Self-pity is a miserable condition in which a person thinks he is the center of the world and that everybody must worship him, and if they do not, he cries. Self-pity must be annihilated because if a person has self-pity, he cannot believe in God. Self-pity imprisons and encapsulates the Self for purposes of the ego.

Self-examination helps us to recognize our own vanities. When I was little, I learned to play the violin. I learned the Hungarian Rhapsody, which I thought I played perfectly. My father came to me while I was practicing one day and said, "Prepare yourself to go out; I have a surprise for you." "Okay, Daddy," I said, "but first sit down and listen to me play." When I finished, he said, "Wonderful! Now get ready so we can go." He took me to a music center where four very fine professionals played the Hungarian Rhapsody. At first I was disgusted, but as I listened, I slowly sank deeper and deeper into the chair. I wanted to disappear. "If this is music," I thought, "then what kind of musician am I?" When we arrived home I told my father that I did not want to play anymore. "That was not the purpose of taking you to the concert," he said. "I wanted you to see the difference between perfection and imperfection."

From that date on, I practiced daily for three to four hours. My mother finally said, "That's enough! I am going crazy!" My father came to me and told me to stop because everybody was complaining. But those four musicians continued to haunt me.

You can work toward perfection by comparing yourself with Christ and seeing what you are. This is how you can change yourself. It is a clear tactic to find the difference between perfection and yourself.

When I was a student of mechanical engineering, I had to work with a very complex piece of machinery that oiled all the wheels of a locomotive engine. My teacher told me to disassemble it and then reassemble it. I disassembled it, but it seemed impossible to put all five hundred pieces back together. I could not remember how I started or where I ended, and I put everything back together in the wrong place. My teacher returned, and re-assembled it correctly in half an hour. I then understood what it meant to have a teacher.

You are going to bring yourself closer to an ideal, to a situation, to a condition which challenges and evokes perfection from you. Only then do you become somebody. But as you become greater and greater, you must always maintain your humility.

The blue flame of love stands for Christ, for the second principle of love and compassion. It has many names, but it is the same thing — practical love. You say, "I love you, honey-bunny," and then one year later, you hate the person. What kind of love is that? What is the practical expression of love in our lives?

The blue flame is love. In the Bible we read,

> *I may speak in the tongues of men and angels, but if I am without love, I am a sounding gong or a clanging cymbal. I may have the gift of prophecy and know every hidden truth; I may have faith strong enough to move mountains. But if I have no love, I am nothing.*
>
> *Love is patient, kind, and envies no one. Love is never boastful, nor conceited, nor rude, never selfish, nor quick to take offense. Love keeps no score of wrongs; it does not gloat over other men's things, but delights in truth. There is nothing love cannot face. There is no limit to its faith, hope and endurance.*[1]

Perhaps you have heard it said that God is love, and that it is only through love that you can communicate with God and with your fellow man. Test this principle and see how understanding does not

---

1.   I Corinthians 13:1-7

come until a moment when you love another. You will see that when you love each other, any problems between you completely evaporate.

Love solves problems and helps you understand each other. Understanding is not reached, however, when you sit and philosophize about it. Why play games? Love is a straight line from heart to heart. It saves time, money, court costs — everything. Get to the bottom line and say, "I love you," and mean it, or there is no love.

The greatest expression of love is tolerance. The word "tolerance" has a very important meaning, but it is a very dangerous word if it is used incorrectly. If you misunderstand it, you will say, "My daughter is a prostitute, but I am very tolerant." This is not an example of tolerance. In tolerance you do not share the shortcomings of other people, neither do you encourage them in their weaknesses. But you do not hate them, and you always make your light and service available to them when they need you. Tolerance does not impose; it illuminates and challenges.

The yellow flame is the symbol of light. This is the light of pure intelligence, pure reasoning, and pure logic. If you have this light, then you have pure logic in your business, in family matters, in all your relationships. You do not fall into self-deception.

Most of us deceive ourselves; it is such a pleasant game to deceive ourselves and feel happy. Watch your life closely to see how you deceive yourself. Sometimes you are under the misconception that you do not have this problem. But your transformation starts the moment you see how you deceive yourself. The mind especially deceives you. Your emotions, your stomach, and your sex drives deceive you. It is important to find out how and when they deceive you because when this is discovered, the light of the yellow flame increases. You develop understanding and a light that sees things as they actually are. There is no fabrication — only clear vision. When you are approaching a problem and trying to solve something or trying to build a relationship, do not walk the path of deception.

Self-deception is the result of the absence of the yellow flame. Observe how your mind sometimes fabricates things, and how, instead of stopping the mind, you follow it. You deceive, cheat, and mislead others; but when you deceive, cheat, and mislead yourself, you are in self-deception. This is only the surface; there are deeper and deeper aspects. For example, sometimes we think, "God only loves me and nobody else." Pay attention and try to discover how you are deceiving yourself. If you pay attention, you will gradually minimize self-deception until it no longer exists. Then see how your light will increase.

If your light increases, you will be smarter, clearer, and more up-to-date in school, in business, in society, in your duties and responsibilities. If you are not up-to-date, it is because you distorted your intellectual machinery. You know that your car needs unleaded gas, but you put regular gas in the tank and then complain that the car does not run well. Lies and deception are the wrong fuel. So think clearly, feel clearly, act clearly, decide clearly —

without self-deception — and see how your health improves.

Most sickness is the result of self-deception because every deception conducts the wrong current of energy into the network of your etheric body. If your etheric body receives conflicting commands and has conflicting circuits with conflicting energy flowing into it, you will not be healthy. A healthy man is one who is unified, whole. When Christ said, "If your eye is single, your whole body will be filled with light," He was misunderstood. Singleness means that when you say, "Yes," you mean yes, and that when you say, "No," you mean no. But if you deceive people, your body will be sick. To improve your body, try to remove deceit from yourself. With deceit you push the wrong buttons on the computer and get the wrong results — while expecting the right results. If you push the wrong buttons, do not expect to get the right results.

When your light increases, your flame increases; you read the hearts of people. The Masters always read our hearts. They know what is going on because the light registers everything that is going on like a seismograph.

Those who have light have direction — a light on the path. If you are in darkness, you do not know where you are going. If you see someone who has no direction, instead of saying, "You have no direction, " you can say, "You do not have light." If you give light to him, he will be able to see that there is a door and there is a window. By doping yourself, cheating people, drinking all day and all night, and

214 The Flame of the Heart

lying to your family, you do not have light. If you had light, you would not do these things because **right does not exist when light does not exist**. Light and righteousness go together.

"Direction" is to go toward improvement and perfection in everything that you are doing that aids in your perfection. You can even perfect yourself through your business, through your work.

While in a monastery, the Teacher said to me, "You are going to dig a trench here." When I asked him how long the trench should be, he said, "Just start digging, and I will tell you when to stop." The first day I dug ten feet, but the Teacher said, "That is not enough; tomorrow dig another ten feet." "Why did I come to this school?" I thought. This process continued until I had dug a forty-foot trench — and it still was not enough. "What in the world are you going to do with this trench?" I asked him. "If you don't like it, my son," he said, "get lost. You came here to learn." "Yes, sir," I said, and continued digging.

I dug for several weeks. At night my shoulders were so tired from digging they would not work. Then suddenly I remembered something my father said: "Do everything as if you were doing it for the Lord." I said to myself, "I must dig with love!" The next day before I started I said, "Okay, God, this is for You. This is for Your Angel; this is for Your Holy Spirit; this is for Your Martyrs." There was so much energy in this joy! When the Teacher came to me and said, "I need another four feet," I said with enthusiasm, "Yes, sir!" I had found the secret. So he said, "You do not need to dig anymore."

I used digging for my own perfection. I tested my joy, and when the month was over and I stood before the mirror, I could not believe what muscles I had, how nice my body looked. When I went swimming, people would comment on my muscles. "Yes," I would say, "you must ask me how I did it.

In the *Upanishads* it is said, "I love my children not because of my children, but because the One Self exists in them. I do my job and responsibilities not for the sake of the job or the responsibilities, but for the One Self. In Him we live and move and have our being." This is direction.

When you live on the path of truth, when you have light, the mysteries, the secrets, the laws and principles of God or Nature slowly reveal themselves to you. Great Ones look for the flame in the heart when They choose Their disciples to see how great this flame is. When it is really developed, They say, "Come and join Us at the table of Our feast." This symbolism is found in the Round Table of King Arthur and the flaming Chalice.

The following exercises may help you to increase your aspiration and the power of visualization. These will kindle your heart center.

Visualization B

1. Close your eyes. Visualize a wheel with seven spokes in front of your face. The wheel is red, the spokes are blue, and the hub is yellow. Try to see this and not just imagine it. If you can see the colors and the shape, it is visualization, not imagination.

2. See the colored wheel turn from right to left. Now stop the wheel and keep it in front of your face.

3. Let the outside red circle turn left, the blue spokes right, and the yellow axis left.

4. Continue this visualization for five minutes.

5. Make the wheel disappear. Rub your hands, touch your face, and open your eyes.

Visualization C

1. Close your eyes.

2. See a beautiful flame one foot above your head.

3. See the three colors of the flame — red, blue, and yellow — mixing and fusing with each other like a spiral moving upward.

4. Now visualize that you are in a dark room, sitting in total darkness, and that your flame is really shining.

5. See the light of the flame spreading around your body as you sit in the fire of the flame.

6. Wherever there is a problem in your body, let the flame briefly touch there for not more than one second, purifying and healing everything in your body.

7. Slowly move the flame within your body, and see how the body is like a chalice around the flame. It is good if you feel hot.

8. Visualize that the heat, the fire, and the light of the flame are penetrating and radiating out of your body for a distance of ten feet, purifying everything in your being.

9. Again see the red flame, the blue flame, and the yellow flame. The yellow flame purifies the lymphatic system; the blue flame purifies the blood; the red flame purifies the nervous system.

10. Rub your hands, touch your face, and open your eyes.

Sometimes the flame of the heart is extinguished. The heart then becomes like a stone, like a cave where no love or compassion exists. Such people are found in the history of humanity. Hitler, murderers, rapists, and other criminals have a heart center that is dead, a heart that is crystallized and atrophied. It becomes like wood; the flame is gone. The instant that the flame begins to decrease, man enters into darkness, into the dark path of crime, because he is no longer in touch with higher forces. He becomes an extinguished lamp, and he cannot meet his duties, obligations, or responsibilities and eventually turns against himself. Great Initiates can see when this light is getting smaller; They know when this happens that the man is going to commit suicide or destroy others. Man is in great danger when this light is gone.

We see this happen in families. Suddenly a person is no longer sensitive; he becomes like a stone with no feeling. This eventually leads to separation, divorce, or many other complications. How does this happen?

The first thing that hurts the flame is hatred. Hatred is a great poison that spreads throughout the nervous system, then proceeds to the root of the flame where it consumes the source of energy of the flame.

The second danger is the spirit of revenge. A person may say, "Just wait, I will show you!" but when he does this, he destroys his own flame. It is better to die than to lose the flame. If you die, you die for one life. But if you lose the flame, you are lost for many lives. It is such a tragedy.

Jealousy is the third element which causes damage to the flame. It attacks the flame like a whirlwind and sometimes extinguishes it.

The commission of crime, whether big or small, accumulates like a great storm and threatens the flame. The flame, of course, has its own resistance, being fed from higher sources, and tries to maintain itself. But if the practice of crime continues, the flame eventually disappears.

Treason is disastrous to the flame of the heart, whether it is treason against your family, your country, human rights, or freedom. Never violate the freedom of others so long as they are not using their "freedom" against your freedom.

Malice, or intent to harm, is a direct dose of poison that is injected into the system of others — and gossip is just as bad. Can you hold your tongue? Slandering people's names for your own benefit or for the benefit of others is a heavier form of gossip. Such a person sells his Master or his Teacher for a few dollars, a Judas who says, "Give me thirty pieces of silver and I will betray Him." We do this to each other all the time and think nothing of it. Once during a conversation, a man bragged to me that he had never betrayed anyone in his life. "Well," I said, "you are lying. I saw you at the beach passionately kissing another girl. Isn't this betrayal of your wife?" "Did you see?" he said.

Another thing that really harms the flame is continuous irritation — at home with your children, with your husband or wife, in your job, in your place of worship. Continuous irritation kills your system by creating a poison in your nervous system called imperil.[2] Imperil accumulates in the nerve channels and works its way toward the heart. From the heart, it attacks the flame — and when the flame is attacked, sickness and disease take place in the body because the only protection for the body lies in the flame of your heart. This is where science and religion meet. If you are pure in heart, you will see God within you: beauty, happiness, and victory — everything that God represents.

---

2. For further information, please refer to *The Psyche and Psychism*, Chapter 27, "Irritation — The Destructive Fire."

The poison of irritation is very powerful and deadly. Great Ones tell us not to increase this poison in our system or in the system of others because by irritating others we become responsible for their health.

These kinds of things slowly, gradually kill the flame, and the person is left without light. He had such a beautiful candle, but now it is gone and he is left to sit in darkness. We should not have to sit in darkness.

M.M. says that the flame of the heart is the cure for all diseases. I knew a woman who had severe arthritis in her hand which caused her a tremendous amount of pain and suffering, and she could barely use it. I recommended that she visualize a flame, a beam of light going to her hand, dissipating everything that was foreign in it. She appeared several days later at an evening lecture, and when I asked if there were any questions, she raised her hand and said, "No, but look at my hand!" People thought she was joking, but the flame of her heart helped to heal her hand. Practice this sincerely and see what happens. God gives us everything we need to survive. But first we must know how to visualize, how to be patient, and to understand that karma plays a role.

You can immediately see in a person's eyes if he lacks the flame. It is important to learn the science of the eyes. Look into eyes carefully; what do they say? Is there a flame present? Is there life, or are they dead? Are they clean and pure, or is something else present? The flame of the heart literally can be seen in the eyes. Like the eyes of a cat, the eyes flame when the flame of the heart is present. These are the eyes that influence people. The warmth, the electricity, the radiation of these eyes lead, uplift, and heal people.

When the flame is gone, the following conditions will manifest:

1. Obsession and possession start in your nature. Dark entities may take over your body in three primary locations: the sex center, the solar plexus center, and the throat center. When they enter the sex center, for instance, they stimulate you beyond your capacity and drive you crazy. This is what happened to most of our children in the '60's. They shouted, "Love," but what they got was gonorrhea, syphilis, and later AIDS because their flame was reduced. AIDS is nothing else but the absence of the flame; the vitality of the flame is gone.

Possession is worse because the entity takes over completely and throws the human soul out, using the body for its own interests. You become the embodiment of evil; degenerative diseases and cancer may start appearing in your body. You become a tyrant, a totalitarian, imposing your will and direction on others with fabricated reasons. It is important to watch for these signs.

2. Your eyesight and hearing deteriorate. When you proceed on the path of evil, your eyes will suddenly need three or four changes in prescription. This is a sign that you are doing something wrong. Of course, eyesight also becomes weak from stress, from incorrect diet, or it is inherited from your parents. But be careful if you are young, especially in the mid-teen years, and you suddenly feel blindness.

3. Friendships end. The end of friendship is another sign that something is wrong, that there is something wrong in the heart. This is a sign that the flame is endangered.

4. Prosperity vanishes from your business because the flame is the magnet that draws right money, right prosperity, and right business.

5. You continually fail because something you did caused the flame to diminish. When the flame increases, you become increasingly prosperous, healthy, magnetic, and energetic. But when you engage in crime, you eventually want to die.

We do not want to leave the impression that the flame is totally extinguished when these symptoms occur but that it is decreasing, and its existence is endangered because of the harmful activities of the person.

What, then, are the signs that the flame is increasing in our heart?

The presence of joy is a sign that the light is increasing. If you are gloomy, sad, and depressed, there is something wrong and you need to work harder. Even if something unrighteous happens to you, be joyful. When this happens, think that you are paying for something in a past life.

A thief once broke into my home. The people who discovered the break-in came to me and said,

"He took all of your money." "Well," I said, "I paid something off; payment is now finished." It did not make any difference whatsoever. In the same way, if someone you love dies, do not sit in irritation and curse the laws of God. Say to yourself, "Such things happen; God bless his soul."

It is not possible to say such things if the flame in the heart is not there. When the flame is absent, you sit and become sour, sad, poisonous, and contaminated. But this does not help; instead, you are killing yourself and others. Joy is one of the greatest signs that the flame is increasing within you.

There is so much trash being taught about initiation that we are sometimes ashamed to bring the subject up. The enemies of the Teaching have distorted this subject so much that the real meaning is becoming lost. But we need to understand the meaning of initiation. **Initiation is expansion of consciousness; it is greater understanding and the ability to serve in a greater capacity.** When the flame increases, you take an initiation.

The first initiation is called, in Christian terminology, the Birth of Christ in your heart. You establish contact with Him because the light, the yellow flame, starts to expand and touch the Intuitional Plane. Tradition says that when the flame reaches a certain degree, Christ adds His fire to it, which increases the radiance of your flame. At this initiation you have more abundant love for others, you have a clear direction of life, you have solemnity, you have a sense of responsibility and nobility.

In the first initiation, man tries to live according to the values of spiritual principles. It is a process of perpetual effort. You are not complete; you fall down one hundred times, but you stand up again and say, "I am going to do it."

The second initiation, called purification, is when the blue flame increases. When the fire, the flame of your heart, begins the process of purifying your physical, emotional, and mental bodies, you feel that you are no longer going to say ugly things, think ugly things, feel ugly things. You become tired of being unclean, and you feel like controlling your mouth and your thinking, and your heart and relationships are clean, clean, clean.

In the second initiation, you become

> pure
>
> beautiful
>
> loving

At the Third Initiation, the red flame increases and your entire personality is lit because all the fire latent in every cell and atom in your bodies is released. Clairvoyantly you look just like a Christmas tree.

In the Third Initiation, you develop the following:

> direction
>
> nobility
>
> righteousness

An Initiate of this degree has come from darkness and has become transfigured. When an Initiate goes through Transfiguration, we say that the person has become a Son of Light.

The Doctrine of Heart

There are natural divisions in humanity, such as:

1. Climatic and territorial divisions

2. Color divisions

3. Racial divisions

4. National divisions

5. Divisions into specializations, such as the seven fields of human endeavor

6. Divisions between those who are materialistic, and those who strive toward the spiritualization of humanity and life

There are also higher divisions, for example, in those who form a particular center in the body of the Planetary Soul. These center-divisions are

Head Center

Ajna Center

Throat Center

Heart Center

Solar Plexus Center

Sacral Center

Base of Spine Center

These centers are formed by people irrespective of the initial, general divisions to which they belong.

There are still higher divisions, such as Ray divisions and divisions of Initiations. It is interesting that the higher divisions move toward cooperation and synthesis.

Lower divisions ordinarily live and survive by exploiting and suppressing each other.

All natural divisions are good provided that they see how helpful such divisions can be if they cooperate and contribute to the Common Good. We can have national divisions which result in chaotic, painful conditions all over the world.

We can also have national divisions which result in cooperation, peace, and prosperity on this planet.

Divisions can help further the evolution of humanity or retard its evolution. But if those in higher divisions would explain the reasons for divisions, it would be possible to save humanity on this planet.

The world is one body, one mechanism. Every division mentioned previously is a part in that mechanism, individually and collectively. If these parts do their duty and responsibility, having in their mind the good of the whole body or mechanism, then the whole body can function in a healthy way and each part can benefit from the integrity and health of the whole body.

Suppose that body is a man. How will that man live, serve, and create if his organs and centers are fighting against each other, and, conversely, how will that man grow and bloom if his parts cooperate and are healthy and have the vision of synthesis?

One day we will realize that those who emphasized divisions and used them to have people stand against one another created all the suffering, pain, and retardation that we see in the world.

The heart is the symbol of unification and synthesis. The children in the world must be educated in the following:

1. Each of them has a heart.

2. The heart provides energy and nourishment to every cell in the body.

3. The heart is the distributor of the energy of cooperation and understanding.

4. Every living form has a heart.

5. Every heart feels pain and joy.

6. Every heart is thirsty for love and joy.

7. Every heart is connected with all hearts that exist in the world.

8. All hearts are related to *the Heart which is the heart of all living forms on this earth.*

9. Humanity is a center, or an organ, as are the other kingdoms in the Body of that Heart.

10. The supreme responsibility of each individual and each division is to care for the health of that Great Heart, which is the Center of the Body that is formed by all individual and collective divisions.

Once such a vision is given to the children in the world, in a few decades they will dump all the trash that we created through our separative, destructive, and selfish thinking and will bring in the Age of Synthesis, Cooperation, and Unity.

Every noble soul must distribute this Doctrine of Heart all over the world.

The heart is a progressive and living vision. With the inclusiveness of the heart, every division in humanity will find its right place in the mighty synthesis of labor. Every atom, every living form, every man, every division will be used to dissolve the thoughts of separatism and restore the vision of the heart, the vision of Synthesis, Cooperation, and Unity.

Glossary

Ageless Wisdom: The sum total of the Teachings given by great Spiritual Teachers throughout time. Also referred to as the Ancient Wisdom, the Teaching, the Ancient Teaching.

Arhat: Ancient term designating a person whose consciousness is focused in the Intuitional Plane — a Fourth Degree Initiate.

Aspirant: One who has taken the first initiation — indicated by an intensive struggle to grow into the spiritual life, to follow the way of determined orientation to the things of the spirit, and to live by the light of that spirit.

Astral body: The vehicle composed of astral substance; that through which the emotional aspect of humanity expresses itself. Also known as the subtle body and the emotional body.

Aura: The sum-total of all emanations from all the vehicles of any living thing.

Bhagavad Gita: One section of an epic poem called the *Mahabharata*. The story of the warrior-hero Arjuna — his conflicts, struggles, and his dialogue with his Inner Guide, Krishna. The story symbolizes the unfolding human soul at the transition stage toward Self-awareness.

Center: Any energy vortex found in a human, planetary, or solar body.

Central Spiritual Sun: The Core of the Solar System. The Sun is triple: it includes the visible Sun, the Heart of the Sun, and the Central Spiritual Sun.

Chalice: Also known as the Lotus. Found in the second and third subplanes (from the top) of the mental plane. Formed of twelve different petals of energy: three knowledge petals, three love petals, three sacrifice petals. The innermost three petals remain folded for ages. They are the dynamic sources of these outer petals. The Lotus contains the essence of all of a person's achievements, true knowledge, and service. It is the dwelling place of the Solar Angel.

Chohan: A person who has accomplished the Sixth Initiation.

Continuity of consciousness: A state of consciousness in which you are aware on all levels of the mind and of the higher and lower planes simultaneously.

Core: The essence or Spark of God within each being; the Monad.

Disciple: A person who tries to discipline and master his threefold personality and manifests efficiency in the field where he works and serves.

Fourth Cosmic Ether: An electrical sphere called Intuitional or Buddhic Plane — reached as a result of the transmutation process of man's progression on the Path.

Fourth Initiation: The Crucifixion Initiation during which the Solar Angel leaves and the Chalice is destroyed by the fully awakened Jewel or Core.

Great Ones: Beings who have taken the Fifth Initiation or beyond. See Masters.

Hierarchy: The members of the spiritual Hierarchy have triumphed over matter and have complete control of the personality, or lower self. Its members are known as Masters of Wisdom Who are custodians of the Plan for humanity and all kingdoms evolving within the sphere of Earth. It is the Hierarchy that translates the Purpose of the Planetary Logos into a Plan for all kingdoms of the planet.

Higher Worlds: Those planes of existence that are of a finer vibration of matter than the physical plane. Generally refers to the higher mental plane and above.

Human soul: See soul.

Initiate: A person who has taken an initiation. See also Initiation.

Initiation: The result of the steady progress of a person toward his life's goals, achieved through service and sacrifice, and manifested as an expansion of one's consciousness. It represents a point of achievement marked by a level of enlightenment and awareness. There are a total of nine Initiations that the developing human soul must experience in order to reach the Cosmic Heart.

Karma, Law of: The Law of Cause and Effect or attraction and repulsion. "As you sow, so shall you reap."

Lotus: Also known as the Chalice. See Chalice.

Masters: Individuals Who had the privilege to master Their physical, emotional, mental, and intuitional bodies.

Mental Body: The vehicle composed of the substance of the mental plane in which humanity expresses itself through thought.

Mind, higher and lower: See Planes.

Monad: See Self.

Personality: The three vehicles of man. The combined forces and vehicles in which the evolving human soul expresses himself and gains experience during incarnation. These vehicles are the physical body, the emotional or astral body, and the mental body.

Plan: The formulation of the Purpose of the Planetary Logos into a workable program — a Plan — by the Planetary Hierarchy for all kingdoms of nature.

Planes: There are seven planes through which a human being travels and which make up human consciousness. From the lowest level upward, they are called: Physical, Emotional or Astral, Mental, Intuitional or Buddhic, Atmic, Monadic, Divine. Each plane is subdivided into seven planes. The first three subplanes of the mental plane from the bottom are numbers seven, six, and five, which form the lower mental plane. Number four is the middle mind or link. Numbers three, two, and one form the higher mental plane.

Purpose: That which the Solar Logos is intended to achieve at the end of the evolution of the Solar System. The Plan is the formulation of this Purpose for our planet only.

self: The small "s" self is the sumtotal of the physical, emotional, and mental bodies of man. Commonly called the "lower self" or personality.

Self: The capital "S" Self is another term used to refer to the Core of the human being. The True Self is the developing, unfolding human soul who is trying to liberate himself, go back to his Father, and become his True Self.

Shamballa: Known as the White Island, it exists in etheric matter and is located in the Gobi Desert. Shamballa is the dwelling place of the Lord of the World, Sanat Kumara, and is the place where "the Will of God is known." It is a sphere of energy which transmits interplanetary and solar directions to the Hierarchy, and periodically to humanity, thus keeping the planetary lives in tune with solar directions.

Silver thread: Also known as the life thread — the connecting link between the heart and Monad. It is anchored in the etheric heart center.

Solar Angels: Very advanced beings who sacrificed Their life, descending from Higher Worlds to help the evolution of humanity and guide its steps toward initiation. This happened on our planet at the middle of the Lemurian period. They are also called Guardian Angels.

soul: The small "s" soul is the human psyche, the Spark, traveling on the path of evolution and having three powers: willpower, attraction, and intelligence to guide its development. Also known as the evolving human soul.

Soul: Also known as the Solar Angel.

Soul-infused personality: A state in which the physical, emotional, and mental bodies are purified to a high degree and aligned with the Solar Angel so that the light of the Solar Angel can radiate through the personality in full power and beauty.

Spark: Human Monad fallen into matter.

Spiritual Triad: The field of awareness of the human soul. This field comes into being when the magnetic fields of the Mental Permanent Atom, the Buddhic Permanent Atom, and the Atmic Permanent Atom fuse and blend.

Subtle World: The astral plane.

Teaching, Sacred: See Ageless Wisdom.

Third Initiation: The total purification and alignment of the mental, emotional, and physical vehicles of the evolving human soul, leading to Transfiguration or Enlightenment.

Thousand-petaled Lotus: The head center which takes the place of the Chalice after the fourth Initiation.

Transcendental Self: The Solar Angel, the Inner Guide.

Transfiguration: The result of the action of the electric fire of the Spiritual Triad on the higher mind. The lights in the little atoms of the personality vehicles are released, and the whole personality is purified in the Third Initiation.

Transformation: The result of the action of solar fire on the astral body. The astral body comes under the influence of the Solar Angel and the Intuitional Plane.

Transmutation: The result of the action of the fire of mind on the physical body. The physical body comes under the control of the human soul.

True Self: See Self.

Vanity: Vanity is illusion based on egotistical pride of the personality. In essence, vanity is clothing an opinion of ourselves with a distorted perception of facts. It is a state of being wherein we think we are something which we are not; know something which we do not know; have something which we do not have; are able to do something which we are incapable of doing. It exists in mental matter in the aura and is fed by and through the personality.

"Voice of Silence": Also known as the Inner Voice. The Inner Voice is higher than the conscience. It is the Real Voice talking within you. It is direct communication with your Solar Angel.

Upanishads: Mystical treatises forming the Divine Revelation of the scriptures of the Hindus, said to date approximately from the Sixth Century, B.C. The *Upanishads* are said to be the source of all six systems of Hindu philosophy.

Bibliographic References

Agni Yoga Society. New York: Agni Yoga Society.
  Aum, 1959.
  Community, 1951.
  Heart, 1982.
  Hierarchy, 1977.
  Infinity, Vol. I, 1980.

Bailey, Alice A. New York: Lucis Publishing Company.
  A Treatise on Cosmic Fire, 1951, 1977.

Lamsa, George M., trans. Philadelphia: A. J. Holman Co. Bible Publishers.
  The New Testament, 1968.

Saraydarian, Torkom. Sedona, AZ: Aquarian Educational Group.
  Challenge For Discipleship, 1986.
  The Psyche and Psychism, 1981.
  The Science of Becoming Oneself, 1976, 1982.
  The Science of Meditation, 1981.

Saraydarian, Torkom. West Hills, CA: T.S.G. Publishing Foundation, Inc.
  Other Worlds, 1990.

About The Author

This is Torkom Saraydarian's latest published book. Many more will be released very soon. His vocal and instrumental compositions number in the hundreds and are being released.

The author's books have been used all over the world as sources of guidance and inspiration for true New Age living based on the teachings of the Ageless Wisdom. Some of the books have been translated into other languages, including German, Dutch, Danish, Portuguese, French, Spanish, Italian, Greek, Yugoslavian, and Swedish. He holds lectures and seminars in the United States as well as in other parts of the world.

Torkom Saraydarian's entire life has been a zealous effort to help people live healthy, joyous, and successful lives. He has spread this message of love and true vision tirelessly throughout his life.

From early boyhood the author learned first-hand from teachers of the Ageless Wisdom. He has studied widely in world religions and philosophies. He is in addition an accomplished pianist, violinist, and cellist and plays many other instruments as well. His books, lectures, seminars, and music are inspiring and offer a true insight into the beauty of the Ageless Wisdom.

Torkom Saraydarian's books and music speak to the hearts and minds of a humanity eager for positive change. His books, covering a large spectrum of human existence, are written in straightforward, unpretentious, clear, and often humorous fashion. His works draw on personal experiences, varied and rich. He offers insight and explanations to anyone interested in applying spiritual guidelines to everyday life. His no-nonsense approach is practical, simple, and readily accessible to anyone who is interested in finding real meaning in life.

Torkom Saraydarian has de-mystified the mysteries of the Ageless Wisdom. He has made the much needed link between the spiritual and the everyday worlds. Look for his exciting new books and music being released.

Index

239

See also Vices
Group
  and closed heart, 176
  and flame of heart, 74
  defined, 150
Group consciousness, 73
Group love
  defined, 45
  how manifested, 74
Group membership
  defined, 150
Groups, best
  and heart, 140
Guilt
  and effect on heart, 176
  defined, 179

ℋ

Happiness, 107, 126, 139, 143,
  157, 168, 179, 201, 219
Harmfulness
  defined, 74
Harmlessness, 71, 73-74, 147,
  171, 179
  and heart, 137
  use in developing heart, 131
Hate
  effect on person, 159
Hateful thoughts
  effects of, 45
Hatred, 17, 19, 21, 40, 42-44, 46,
  49, 66, 105-106, 141, 145, 154,
  156, 158, 176, 192-193
  and energy, 42
  and flame, 218
  cause and effect of, 43
  See also Vices
Healer, unseen, 31
Healing
  and compassion, 62
  and consciousness, 33
  and cosmic energies, 30, 34
  and flame of the heart, 34
  and heart, 31, 52
  and Hierarchy, 33
  and pure heart, 20
  and virtues, 116

  by flame of heart, 220
  by heart, 195
  by visualization exercise, 216
  evocation of, 33
  with virtues, 112
Healing rays
  and Hierarchy, 35
Healing, of heart
  and compassion, 69
Healing, power of, 71
Healing, psychic, 162
  and color, 126
Health
  and color image, 126
  and heart, 22, 139
  and Transfiguration, 71
  how improves, 213
  how restored, 44
  of three bodies, 193
Health and healing
  and cleavages, 40
Health, future
  and psychic energy, 34
Health, improvement of
  and use of color, 127
Health, of body
  benefits of, 229
Hearing
  reason for weakness, 221
Heart
  ailments of, 28
  and absorbtion of mind, 108
  and agreement of, 52
  and beauty, 105
  and communication, 18, 23, 58,
  154-155
  and conquering, 23
  and Cosmic Life, 68
  and courage, 52
  and creativity, 18
  and decisions, 11
  and development of exercises,
  130-131
  and direction, 56
  and doingness, 204
  and elements of pollution, 19
  and enthusiasm, 164
  and Essence, vii, 56

Light, love, power
  and heart, 29
Light, primordial, 170-171
Light, shining
  qualities of, 206
Light, Son of, 225
Light, yellow flame of, 211
Limitations
  kinds of, 145
Logic, pure, 171
Lotus, viii, 69-70, 197
Lotus of the Heart, 160
Lotus, flaming
  defined, 190
  See also Chalice
Love, viii, 12, 16-17, 21, 29-30,
  36, 40-46, 62-64, 66-67, 72-75,
  78, 80, 85, 88-92, 101, 108,
  111, 117, 125, 140, 143,
  146-147, 151, 156-158, 167,
  171, 179, 183, 186, 190, 192,
  195, 198, 204, 207-208,
  210-212, 214-215, 217, 221,
  223, 230
  and communication, 42
  and development of heart, 98
  and etheric centers, 41
  and healing of heart, 53
  and heart, 16, 58, 157
  and problem solving, 211
  and synthesis, 44
  as path of transformation, 42
  See also Heart
  right use of, 91
Love, Divine, 197
Love, energy of
  result of absence, 40
Love, group
  how created, 45
Love, true
  source of, 42
Love, unlimited, 146
Love-wisdom
  and heart center, 41
Lymphatic system
  purification of, 217

M

M.M.
  from *Heart*, vi
  on cancer, 20
  on heart as cure, 220
  on Helena Roerich, 145
  on Karma, 177
  See also Quotes
  Temple of the Heart, iii
Magnet
  and virtues, 115
Magnetism, 107, 142, 175
  and virtues, 18, 115
  increase of, 18
Malice
  and flame, 219
Man, average
  consciousness of, 37
Man, noble
  consciousness of, 37
Manipulation, 177
  and lack of virtue, 173
Master
  how to become, 59
Masters, 172
  and light of soul, 127
  and reading hearts, 213
  as human beings, 129
Materialism, 74
  defined, 88
Maya, 169
Measure, correct
  and humility, 76
Medical profession
  and health of heart, 193
Medicine, future
  basis of, 43
Meditation, 31, 42, 172
  and heart development, 98
  and Hierarchy, 34
  and path to heart, 137
  on compassion, 63
Memory
  and heart, 69
Mental
  See also Bodies and personality

S

and karmic debts, 113
and readiness for labor, 118
and senses of the heart, 156
as pure water, 121
how to have, 165
list for meditation, 161
source of, 100
Virtues, levels of
and how to use, 160
Virtues, of heart
function of, 112
Virtues, twelve
and Disciples, 115
and heart petals, 20
Vision, actualization of
and virtues, 116
Visionaries
and fools, 96
Visualization
on flame and colors, 216
on wheel and colors, 215
to improve sensitivity to effect
of flame, 40, 195
vs. imagination, 215
Vitality
and use of color, 125
Vivisection, 176
"Voice of Silence"
as agent of communication, 130

W

Wars
and museums, 16
causes of, 84
how to stop, 158
Wealth
and virtues, 114
Wholeness
and heart, 58
Wife, best
and commitment, 61
Will
and beauty, 105
Will aspect
how emerges, 104
Will, Divine
and labor, 78

how evoked, 105
Willpower, 198
Will, pure
manifestation of, 100
Wisdom, 11, 17, 28, 45, 66, 105,
153, 161, 170-171, 173, 199
and spiritual identification, 79
components of, 171
defined, 80
source of, 168
ways to acquire, 172
Wisdom and heart
defined, 66
Wisdom, "heavenly", 173
Wisdom, hidden, 172
Wisdom, schools of
qualities, 174
Wisdom, theoretical, 173
Women
role in education, 16
World, betterment of
through wisdom, 174
World, changes in
and using heart, 206
World, regeneration of, 186
Worship
and pure heart, 23

Y

Year 2000, 192
Yellow
and Chalice colors, 197-198

Z

Zodiacal signs
seven energies of, 29

Other Books
by Torkom Saraydarian

The Ageless Wisdom
The Bhagavad Gita
Breakthrough to Higher Psychism
Challenge For Discipleship
Christ, The Avatar of Sacrificial Love
A Commentary on Psychic Energy
Cosmic Shocks
Cosmos in Man
Dialogue With Christ
Flame of Beauty, Culture, Love, Joy
Hiawatha and the Great Peace
The Hidden Glory of the Inner Man
I Was
Joy and Healing
Legend of Shamballa
Other Worlds
The Psyche and Psychism
The Psychology of Cooperation and Group Consciousness
The Purpose of Life
The Science of Becoming Oneself
The Science of Meditation
The Sense of Responsibility in Society
Sex, Family, and the Woman in Society
Spiritual Regeneration
The Solar Angel
Symphony of the Zodiac
Talks on Agni
Triangles of Fire
Unusual Court
Woman, Torch of the Future
The Year 2000 & After

Vision Series Next Release: **Dynamics of Success**

Booklets by
Torkom Saraydarian

A Daily Discipline of Worship
Fiery Carriage and Drugs
Five Great Mantrams of the New Age
Hierarchy and the Plan
Irritation — The Destructive Fire
Questioning Traveler and Karma
Spring of Prosperity
Synthesis
Torchbearers
Responsibility
The Psychology of Cooperation
Building Family Unity
The Responsibility of Fathers
The Responsibility of Mothers
What to Look for in the Heart of Your Partner

Ordering Information

Write to the publisher for additional information regarding:

—Free catalog of author's books and music tapes

—Information regarding lecture tapes and videos

—Placement on mailing list

—Information on new releases

Additional copies of *The Flame of the Heart*
U.S. $12.95
Postage within U.S.A. $2.50
Plus applicable state sales tax

T.S.G. Publishing Foundation, Inc.
Visions for the Twenty-First Century

Visions for the 21st Century®
P.O. Box 7068
Cave Creek, AZ 85331-7068 U.S.A.
Tel: (602) 502-1909
Fax: (602) 502-0713